Wake Me Up When It's All Over...

Wake Me Up
When It's
All Over...

UNPUBLISHED LETTERS
TO
𝕿𝖍𝖊 𝕯𝖆𝖎𝖑𝖞 𝕿𝖊𝖑𝖊𝖌𝖗𝖆𝖕𝖍

EDITED BY KATE MOORE

Aurum

First published in 2021 by Aurum,
an imprint of The Quarto Group
The Old Brewery, 6 Blundell Street,
London, N7 9BH, United Kingdom

www.QuartoKnows.com/aurumpress

ISBN: 978-0-7112-6891-3
Ebook ISBN: 978-0-7112-6893-7

10 9 8 7 6 5 4 3 2 1

2025 2024 2023 2022 2021

Typeset in Mrs Eaves by SX Composing DTP, Rayleigh, Essex

Printed and bound in Great Britain by Clays Ltd, Elcograf S.p.A.

Jacket Design by Paileen Currie

CONTENTS

INTRODUCTION

What happens after everything stops?

That was the question facing the country as we headed into 2021; and it is one to which the answer is still being written. Like a faltering panellist on *Just a Minute*, this was a year full of hesitation, repetition and deviation. The outstanding success of the Covid-19 vaccination programme failed to secure the swift release from lockdown that some had envisaged. Deadlines were set and then missed; one set of restrictions replaced another. People hurried back to work only to be "pinged" by the NHS Covid-19 app and sent into isolation once more. The public might have been forgiven for wondering whether the Government's "road map" back to normality had gone missing en route.

Thankfully, *Telegraph* readers are made of stern stuff. During uncertain times, they have been an unfailing source of wit, wisdom and resolve. They excel in small, practical solutions to what bureaucrats see as large, intractable problems. Who else would see a parable for the Scottish government in their dealings with two squabbling Jack Russells, or a message for the Sage advisory group in the latest edition of *Gardeners' World*? Whatever the story, the readers can be trusted to find the ridiculous side: indeed, in 2021, this was often the only sane way of looking at events.

After all, this was the year in which the Prime Minister's choice of wallpaper made headline news, and Britain nearly came to blows with the EU over sausages. Joe Biden entered the White House, Jeff Bezos left the Earth and the Sussexes sent increasingly bizzare signals from Planet Hollywood. On the subject of social distancing, the Health Secretary, Matt Hancock, spectacularly failed to practise what he preached. This was also the year in which by-elections – normally reliable ways of annoying the Government – swung both ways. In traditionally red Hartlepool, the Tories trounced Labour – while in true blue Chesham and Amersham, the Liberal Democrats toppled the Tories.

In Covid Britain, many of the ordinary landmarks of life have looked different. Boris Johnson's marriage to the mother of his child took place in secret. The funeral of the Duke of Edinburgh, who died just short of his 100th birthday, took place with royal ceremony but with no crowds – only the statutory congregation of 30. No one attended the Olympic Games – although, in a reassuring return to form, England was thrashed in the cricket and the UK managed a total of *nul points* in the Eurovision Song Contest.

The unusual shape of the year can also be seen in the look of this edition. Letters about summer exploits abroad were, understandably, thin on the ground. Instead, we received regular updates on the view from people's windows. Gardening, nature, homegrown exercise routines and amateur haircuts have all featured prominently. Ever optimistic, readers found things to like about face masks (excellent nose-warmers) and embraced the opportunity for new hobbies in a world of enforced inactivity. They have grappled with the latest rules on physical contact – are cuddles permitted as well as hugs? – and the finer points of Zoom etiquette. Add these to their thoughts on everything from sex and religion to the weather, and you have an idiosyncratic portrait of modern life in all its absurdity.

The hopeful phrase of 2021 has been Freedom Day – hopeful, but elusive. We thought it might come in June. Then it arrived – sort of – in July, with more promised for August. People were still unsure whether or not to remove their masks. But it takes more than PPE and lockdowns to tether free spirits. In their letters to the Editor, *Telegraph* readers have sung like birds in a cage.

My thanks must go to Katie Bond at Quarto, who stepped into the breach after I was "pinged" and confined to quarters as the book neared completion. Thanks also to everyone else at Quarto. At the *Telegraph*, thanks to Rachel Welsh for her legal wisdom, to Matt for his splendid cover illustration; to Michael Stenz and to the Letters Editor, Christopher Howse, for keeping a steady hand on the tiller.

Most importantly, a big thank you to the readers themselves, for being such excellent company throughout the year that was and then wasn't. It has, as ever, been a privilege to rifle through the postbag.

Kate Moore
London SE1

FAMILY
TRIALS AND
TRIBULATIONS

If you can't stand the heat...

SIR — According to an article in the business section, "Kitchens are home to three billion rows a year".

My wife's response to that was, "We obviously don't have rows, as you are never in the kitchen."

Rather unfair, I thought!

John Bryant
Toddington, Bedfordshire

SIR — My wife gets to read the main part of the newspaper while I read the business section. When handed the main part, I noticed that pages 21 and 22 were missing. Later I discovered them in a waste basket — to find that it was Michael Deacon's article on "Why men should do less housework". I suspect that I was not supposed to find this.

Robert Ward
Loughborough, Leicestershire

SIR — Are tins of corned beef designed specifically to injure the person opening them? Asking on behalf of my wife.

Colin Whitfield
Stockton-on-Tees, Co Durham

SIR — For almost 50 years we have had a jar labelled: "What is it?" in a kitchen cupboard.

The contents are odd pieces of metal, plastic, washers, keys, etc.

To date no one has ever been able to identify or find a use for any of these items.

Angela Master
Royston, Hertfordshire

SIR — We were woken yet again in the early hours by the sound of a mountain of books crashing to the floor somewhere in the house. It occurs to me that such top-heavy piles could well prove a deterrent to burglars. They would never be able to negotiate a path to any valuables without causing a cascade.

Not that there are any heirlooms, of course. Just lots of books.

Lesley Thompson
Lavenham, Suffolk

SIR — My local bank manager told me that the three most stressful events in life are moving house, divorce and jumble sales.

Tony Manning
Barton on Sea, Hampshire

A most gallant proposal

SIR — My late husband was rather slow in the proposal department. I knew that things might be reaching fruition when he suggested I attended domestic science classes.

Shirley Copps
Cheltenham, Gloucestershire

SIR – In order to get married next month I now have
to carry out a government-mandated risk assessment.
Isn't that the purpose of courting?

Alastair Prain
London SW9

SIR – My best man whistled the theme from *The Great
Escape* all the way to the church before my wedding.
My wife and I celebrate 40 years of marriage in June.

Laurence Wilbraham
Cawston, Warwickshire

SIR – The evidence points – perhaps surprisingly
for some – to married men living longer. For Ziona
Chana, who died at the relatively young age of only 75,
it seems his 39 wives proved a tad too exhausting and
he is an exception to the rule.

David North-Coombes
Ottershaw, Surrey

Years of service

SIR – During our time in the RAF, a clock, a bookcase
and six wine glasses were added to the contents of
married quarters when the rank of Warrant Officer
was reached. We presumed that the powers that be
considered that by the time that rank was achieved,
service people and their families would have learnt to
read, to tell the time and to not drink out of jam jars.

Linda Fisher
Gloucester

SIR – The advantage of a left-handed wife is that if you seat her to my right my glass is never empty.

Andrew Rollings Red
Hereford

SIR – The head of operations in this household gift-wrapped, most beautifully, a roll of gaffer tape for me to open on Christmas morning. I had asked for some fuse wire.

Alexandra King
Ibthorpe, Hampshire

SIR – My wife never keeps things in case they may be useful in the future. Fortunately she has made an exception in my case.

Julian Tope
Portishead, Somerset

SIR – Annoying habits appear in marriages with old age (I'm 78). For example, my wife complains about me constantly repeating myself. SIR – Annoying habits appear in marriages with old age (I'm 78). For example, my wife complains about me constantly repeating myself. SIR – Annoying habits appear in marriages with old age (I'm 78). For example, my wife complains about me constantly repeating myself. SIR – Annoying habits appear in marriages with old age (I'm 78). For example, my wife complains about me constantly repeating myself. SIR – Annoying habits appear in marriages with old age (I'm 78). For example, my wife complains about me constantly repeating myself. SIR – Annoying habits appear in marriages with old age (I'm 78). For example, my wife complains about me constantly repeating myself. I am sure my wife is mistaken in this. I am sure my wife is mistaken in this. I am sure my wife is mistaken in this. I am sure my wife is mistaken in this.

T. H.
Oulton, Norfolk

Keeping faith

SIR – After the online Sunday church service our vicar has set up a Zoom coffee get-together and he has the ability to "mute" us. My husband commended him on something he had never achieved in nearly 50 years of marriage to me.

Susie Tweed
Long Melford, Suffolk

SIR – Every Ash Wednesday my older brother reminds me that, as a child, I selflessly gave up eating cabbage as my annual Lenten penance. I still do, although I now also eschew the delights of kale.

William T. Nuttall
Rossendale, Lancashire

SIR – I considered giving up watching TV news for Lent.

But realising that watching it really is penance enough, I abandoned the idea.

Edward Pryce
Plymouth, Devon

SIR — I have decided to abstain from the following:

1. Going to the pub
2. Eating out in a restaurant
3. Playing with my grandchildren
4. Inviting my family for Sunday lunch
5. Going to watch my favourite rugby team play

I was wondering. If I give up five things this year, can I have the next four years off?

Grant Jordan
Basingstoke, Hampshire

SIR — The Archbishop of Canterbury is on a sabbatical. I must admit that I hadn't noticed.

Stuart Geddes
Monmouth

Many happy returns

SIR — Those of us who are about to twiddle our thumbs through a second lockdown birthday should be compensated next year.

Between 23 and 28 March 2022, employers and teachers, family and friends should expect a period of high jinks and low productivity from members of this very select club.

They can turn a blind eye or join in the fun, whichever is appropriate.

Anna-Clare Seymour
Wells, Somerset

SIR – A little over 59 years ago, my mother gave birth to me at home. The attending midwife conducted some post-delivery checks, only to declare, "Hold on, there's another bugger in there!" There were no scans back then, and my wholly unexpected brother duly arrived nearly 26 hours later. One of us got the cot; the other a dressing-table drawer.

Keith Edwards
Lincoln

SIR – My father, a keen ornithologist, called his four sons Martin, Peregrine, Jay and Kestrel. My mother always wondered what a daughter might have been named.

My daughter is Robin and she has Osprey and Kite as cousins. I tried to persuade her to call her son Albert Ross but she was not fooled.

Jay Simson
Amberley, West Sussex

SIR – I have two daughters, and I am eternally grateful that I ended up at the ballet and not on a windy football terrace.

Rev Roger Holmes
Howden, East Yorkshire

When your number's up

SIR – I have just signed up to donate my organs.
Interestingly they requested my telephone number.
I'm sure not to answer!

Andrew Potter
Bluntisham, Cambridgeshire

SIR – Now that I am in my mid-eighties I have come
to the conclusion that all my friends of similar age are
in one of the following "d" categories: dead, dotty,
disabled, depressed or deaf. I'm not sure if I'm dotty
but I am deaf.

Mary Valpy
Malvern, Worcestershire

SIR – My hearing not being what it was, I was
interested to hear on the BBC News that this is
Death Awareness Week.

David de Lloyd
Cardiff

SIR – I have often wondered if TV advertising has any
persuasive effect. After watching a plethora of those
pushing funeral plans in which the actors are not just
excited at their own forthcoming demise but thrilled
at being able to pay the bills once they have shuffled
off, I can report that they do work. After seeing so
many I find I have lost the will to live.

Jack Crawford
Solihull, West Midlands

Clean eating

SIR – Last week I bought a packet of cleansing and descaling tablets for the lavatory pan, and noticed on the box that these were suitable for vegans. Could any meat-avoiding readers suggest a recipe, or sauce, to accompany these toilet blocks?

Roy S. Goodman
Ashford, Kent

Abstinence makes the heart grow fonder

SIR – While my daughter remains at home on an extended break from university, it is impossible to maintain a dry January. Besides, a dry February is a better choice. It's a shorter month.

Nigel Algar
Bottesford, Nottinghamshire

SIR – My "dry" January is going so well that I am thinking of extending it into Fe-*brut*-ary and perhaps as far as *Sec*-tember.

James Fraser
Staines-upon-Thames, Surrey

SIR – A lot has been written about parents dealing with children during lockdown – but what of children dealing with octogenarian parents?

I find they are just as likely to misbehave, but the threat of confiscating their respective bottles of sherry and whisky usually does the trick.

Joanna Bunkham
Swansea

SIR – Pubs without beer is an oxymoron. If the Government opens hospitality venues without alcohol the stress will be on the moron.

Victoria Cockburn
Bishop's Castle, Shropshire

SIR – I see a new study has found that strangers who drink alcohol together move closer by 1 centimetre every 3 minutes. That is, 2 metres – the requirement to maintain social distancing – in 6,000 minutes. Even in my student days I never endured a drinking session as long as 100 hours. Obviously the volunteers at the University of Illinois are now made of sterner stuff.

Sir Peter Innes
Winchester, Hampshire

SIR – I was seduced by the idea that natural wine was de rigueur. So I tried some.
I now understand why it fell out of fashion in the first place.

Robin Warde
Duporth, Cornwall

SIR – I will shortly be issued with a blue wheelie bin just to recycle glass. As I do not drink alcohol, my jam jar will feel lonely.

Bernard Powell
Southport, Lancashire

SIR – For service in 1st The Queen's Dragoon Guards in BAOR in the 1980s, the ability to remove the cork from a bottle of champagne with a sword was a necessary skill and rite of passage for all officers on joining the regiment.

But we were completely outclassed by the arrival in the mess of a delegation of French cavalry, who performed the same trick with far greater panache using the base of a champagne flute. On removing the cork with the flute they were half a glass ahead of us, being immediately ready to consume, while we turned to find a glass. We soon changed our approach and customs.

Edward Barham
Rolvenden, Kent

SIR – A few years ago on a touring holiday of the Hebrides we met a doctor from South Wales. He told us, "The golden rule is never to drink more than your GP."

For Christmas he had been given a book entitled *101 Whiskies to Try Before You Die*, and only had a couple more to tick off.

He stated that he had one of the most popular practices in the region.

Stephen Graham
Stockton-on-Tees, Co Durham

The doctor won't see you now

SIR – When I was young I believed in the existence of GPs. They were the nice people who one visited in their grotto called, I believe, The Surgery. There one would be rewarded with nice things to make you feel better. Maybe once a year they would come to your home and, if you had been good, would hand out medicines.

Now I have ceased to believe that they actually exist. The elves in reception still are present but they merely tell you to call back later. It is so sad to have my dreams shattered.

Alan Witt
Charing, Kent

SIR – Telephone consultations with a GP should be placed ahead of chocolate teapots and open-toed wellingtons on a list of the world's most useless things.

Leonard Macauley
Staining, Lancashire

SIR – This morning I phoned our local vet to request repeat medication for my cat. A friendly receptionist quickly arranged for me to pick up the tablets tomorrow. Last week I used an eConsult form to ask my doctor for repeat medication for myself. More than 24 hours later, someone from the surgery called to say my prescription would be ready in 72 hours.

What has my cat done to deserve preferential treatment?

Richard Cheeseman
Yateley, Hampshire

SIR – Reading the debate on the usefulness of video consultations has reminded me of a lesson which was forcefully driven home to me by a well-remembered consultant surgeon at the old Westminster Hospital when I was a medical student.

Berating me for my failure to complete the physical examination of a patient with prostate symptoms, his words were: "Why do you think you come here, Mitchell? We could do all this by correspondence course, but we don't. Do you know why not, Mitchell? Because nobody has ever put their finger into a man's rectum by post yet!"

Andrew Mitchell FRCS
Milton Keynes, Buckinghamshire

SIR – For the emergency listing for telephone numbers on our kitchen notice board I have deleted the reference to "Surgery" and substituted the name "Alcatraz".

Roger W. Powell
Hadzor, Worcestershire

East, west, home's best

SIR – I trust that the Three Kings will be granted permission to travel. Our crib at church is eagerly awaiting their arrival on 6 January.

Louise Huber
Preston, Lancashire

SIR – My neighbour is mowing his lawn, in the first week of February. Is it evidence of climate change, or of lockdown fever?

Bill Welland
Somerton, Somerset

SIR – Is the latest definition of being middle class that you are able to show the world that you have a book-lined study from which to hold your Zoom meetings?

Ted Shorter
Tonbridge, Kent

SIR – During this latest lockdown I have come to suspect that my wife has been secretly adjusting the lavatory seats in our house so that they will not remain vertical unless held in position manually.

Is this grounds for divorce?

Bob Gould
Selsey, West Sussex

SIR – With Valentine's Day in the offing, adverts abound suggesting a "cosy night in". We have just had nearly a year of cosy nights in. What we really want is a riotous night out!

Mike Thomas
Lymington, Hampshire

SIR – May I express my deep disappointment at Lockdown 2: The Sequel. It isn't anywhere near as good as the original.

Simon Hubbard
Brownhills, Staffordshire

Work, rest and play

SIR – Yesterday, having completed my home exercise routine, I created a new word to describe how I felt.

The word is "Smugerred".

Peter Conway
Steyning, West Sussex

SIR – According to my newly acquired Fitbit, ironing is the new swimming. I have already achieved 29 lengths without leaving my sitting room.

Ginny Hudson
Southampton

SIR – I add the tea towels to bulk out my ironing pile, so that once a week I can escape to the lounge with my ironing board. Then I can justify daytime TV watching: an episode of *Perry Mason*, *Father Brown* or *Murder, She Wrote*.

Gillian Gladwin
Great Sutton, Cheshire

SIR – I see in today's edition that a five-minute snooze is recommended. I must warn that this is very optimistic. The last time I tried it, I awoke two hours later.

Tony Waldeck
Truro, Cornwall

Domestic science

SIR – We undergo daily Covid testing by our elderly dog, known affectionately as Professor Sir Martin Jack Russell. Every morning he makes sure we can still smell his halitosis. It probably is as accurate as the lateral flow test.

Mark S. Davies FRCS
Chipping Norton, Oxfordshire

SIR – In light of the Prime Minister's renewed instruction to test ourselves for Covid twice a week I have taken it upon myself to examine the efficacy of the lateral flow tests and come up with the following results. Tap water and tea both produce a negative result. Worcestershire sauce provides a void test. Mango chutney and Diet Coke both test positive. Make of that what you will.

Graham Low
Malpas, Cheshire

Persons of interest

SIR – Thank God for the census. Normally in our household my wife and the two cats are at the top of the pecking order, and I come about seventh after a couple of woodlice and a spider. But for one day, every ten years, I am Person One. I filled the form in with a flourish.

Robin Nonhebel
Swanage, Dorset

SIR – The leaflet accompanying the census letter states, "you can submit your completed questionnaire before 21 March if you know who will be in your household on that day".

As we are in lockdown and obliged to stay at home, we can be fairly certain about who will be in our household in just over a week's time. I have completed our form, but did take the precaution of asking my husband if he had any plans to die before census day.

Luckily he replied in the negative.

Sally Butcher
Salisbury, Wiltshire

SIR – On completing our census form, when I
got to the question asking "What is your sexual
orientation?", it was so tempting to write
"horizontal".

David Tucker
Stokenchurch, Buckinghamshire

Love is in the air

SIR – According to folklore, if you see a robin on
Valentine's Day, you will marry a sailor. If you see
a sparrow you will marry a poor man. If you see a
goldfinch you will marry a millionaire. I saw five
goldfinches in my garden yesterday. I'm single. What
should I deduce from that?

Janet Milliken
Folkestone, Kent

SIR – I have bought Scott's porridge oats for years
now, not only because of its fantastic quality but
because of the hunky Scotsman on the front of
the box.

I nearly stopped dead in my tracks in Waitrose when
I saw their rebrand which included a rather more
inferior man. Who is this strange millennial with
no pecs?!

Gone is the sexy rugged smile, only to be replaced by a zeta male, who looks like he is holding an invisible selfie stick.

Outraged does not even cut it.

Johanna Seccombe
London SW19

SIR – This morning my husband, who has a routine eye test booked with Specsavers in August, received a four-page pre-appointment questionnaire to complete. One of the questions was: "What are your hobbies and interests?"

I suggested his answer should be "Sitting outside the pub watching the girls go by – for which I need 20/20 vision."

Rosemary Ridge
Rowlands Castle, Hampshire

SIR – Rowan Pelling writes that GWMH or "good with my hands" might replace GSOH on men's dating profiles.

Beware, ladies, you may find that GWMH means NSIT – "not safe in taxis".

David Gomme
Cirencester, Gloucestershire

SIR – I was delighted to read that an ancient brothel in Pompeii is re-opening to the public.

Will it be cash only, or will cards be accepted as well?

Mike Bucher
Haddington, East Lothian

A little too much off the top

SIR – When a relative of mine complained that her main problem with lockdown was being unable to get to her hairdresser, I suggested that her husband could do a minor interim trim.

Her reply: "You wouldn't suggest that if you saw what he does to the hedge!"

K. Nesbitt
Ramsey, Isle of Man

SIR – I used to have a fringe. I still have a husband, but only just.

Caroline Blackwell
Edinburgh

SIR – Thank you for printing the picture of Tony Blair; one look at that and my wife decided to cut my hair.

Roy Grimsley
London SE2

SIR – Having clipped many horses over decades, I felt eminently qualified to cut my husband's hair when lockdown kicked in. A quick whizz of the clippers and the job was done with no biting, kicking or sedation.

Kate Graeme-Cook
Brixham, Devon

SIR – My wife has been cutting my hair for more than 60 years. What she had to sweep up afterwards used to fill a dustpan. Sadly, what she has to sweep up these days would easily fit into a matchbox.

Michael Duhig
Bishops Stortford, Hertfordshire

SIR – My barber assiduously kept my eyebrows neatly trimmed. In twelve months of lockdown I have let them flourish and now I cannot wait to go to the pub and show off my "Healeys", as I like to call them.

Geoff Fleming
Heytesbury, Wiltshire

SIR – My barber, noticing the length my hair had achieved during lockdown, informed me of the resurging popularity of the mullet, a haircut known as "business in the front, party at the back". Presumably, this is a consequence of Zoom as the back of the head does not appear on webcam.

Ian Eyres
Oswestry, Shropshire

SIR – The local queues outside the barbers' shops on the morning that lockdown restrictions eased were quite long.

I would imagine the ensuing conversation about where one was taking one's holidays was quite short.

Peter Hamilton
London SE3

Perils of homeworking

SIR – In the early days of the pandemic, with many of us working from home, a request was made to update a weekly whereabouts spreadsheet on the shared drive. I knew it was all getting too much when six weeks in a colleague typed "wtf" instead of "wfh" and lots of people copied and pasted the same without (presumably) spotting the error.

Belinda Robinson
Worthing, West Sussex

SIR – For many, such as my daughter and son-in-law, working from home appears to have subtly morphed into living at the office, with no escape permitted under lockdown. This is not the work–life balance that was envisioned.

Bob Vass
Bollington, Cheshire

SIR – Accounting for unsatisfactory performance
by blaming it on Covid has become a way of life. To
redress this habit I suggest "swear boxes" calling for
contributions of 50p each time it crosses one's mind.

Proceeds to the NHS.

Vernon Phillips
Mere, Wiltshire

SIR – To err is human, to really foul things up needs
a computer.

Barry Hughes
Lytham St Annes, Lancashire

In search of lost time

SIR – Rather late in lockdown I have embarked on
Marcel Proust's *À la recherche du temps perdu*. Fifty pages
into the first five hundred, I noticed with some unease
that this is only the first of seven volumes. However,
I took comfort from the fact that it should see me
through this pandemic – and probably the next.

Dominic Weston Smith
Faringdon, Oxfordshire

SIR – As the tedium of lockdown drags on perhaps
I could remind fellow Scrabble players of the
importance of ensuring their set is ready for when we
can all play again in the flesh.

Today I decided to wash all the letter tiles
individually with a toothbrush.

I then put them to dry on a pad on the Aga, which worked well.

The whole task took up almost half an hour.

If you are really bored, you could add an additional five minutes to the job by washing the pouch as well — I did.

Becks Pearson
Exmouth, Devon

SIR — During a telephone conversation with an old friend, he revealed that at the start of the first lockdown he resolved to collect all his photographs and associated documents and collate them in albums.

Currently his wife is enquiring when she may again be granted access to the dining table and he is about to petition the PM for at least three more lockdowns.

Nicholas Franks
Dorchester

SIR — In years to come, people will ask one another of their great accomplishments during what history will record as The Great Lockdown.

With pride, I will look them in the eye and regale them of completing the quest that's broken better souls than I through the decades: I found 20 songs within the entire back catalogue of the Cocteau Twins which were comprehensible.

Mark Boyle
Johnstone, Renfrewshire

SIR – I am a qualified member of the Stafford branch of Tuneless Choir. After more than a year of no meetings I am woefully out of practice. What do I call the level below tuneless?

Barbara Smith
Stafford

SIR – As the pandemic continues and we are all basically under house arrest with elevated stress levels, at which point can we women legitimately indulge in sulks? The alternative, which is full-blown domestic warfare, is ill-advised in the current situation, as it would result in a rising (male) body count.

If sulks become politically acceptable, we must have a protocol for an exit strategy. Perhaps now is the time for a minister (mistress) of sulks. Being a well-qualified sulker, I offer my services.

Jenny Cobb
Mayfield, East Sussex

SIR – Gone on a long time, haven't they, these lockdowns? I live alone and have started talking to insects.

Rachel Palmer
Rhayader, Radnorshire

A clean break for freedom

SIR – As lockdown restrictions look like they may soon be lifted, social media is abuzz with something called a 30-day spring clean.

That sounds far too arduous. I simply keep a stack of get-well cards to put out when visitors arrive so they think I've been too ill to clean.

Nicola Jane Swinney
Bromley, Kent

SIR – I used to wonder how a battery chicken felt on release.
Now I know.
Yours in the pecking order,

Marjorie E. A. Flinton
Sevenoaks, Kent

SIR – In the coming weeks when Covid-19 restrictions are relaxed, we will learn if it is possible to unspook the herd.

Dr David Slawson
Nairn

SIR – It doesn't matter how long you talk about it, or how many people venture an opinion or worry about grazed knees; you'll never know if you can ride a bike unless you take the stabilisers off.

Roger Fowles
Chatham, Kent

SIR – Dozens of family and friends are cordially invited to my Covid-secure, legally compliant, Easter garden protest.

Christopher Healy
Fridaythorpe, East Yorkshire

Getting together

SIR – As summer approaches, more physical contact will be legal. Forward planning for the consequences might be to increase beds in maternity wards to prevent them being overwhelmed.

Camilla Coats-Carr
Teddington, Middlesex

SIR – Before we discard our protection against Covid-19 we should consider what it also offers. Social distancing might not be practical long-term, but masks would be useful in crowded situations such as public transport.

Masks also might protect us from that nasty import from osculatory France: unsought kisses. I hate having arms flung around me while germ-laden saliva is daubed on my face. The old-fashioned British firm handshake is more to my taste; the Germanic heel click and curt nod, while commendable, is a step too far.

Dr Robert J. Leeming FRCPath
Coventry

SIR – I read that "hugging family and friends is to be allowed from next week". At least it is not being made compulsory.

Mark Stephens
Hungerford, Berkshire

SIR – Hugging's one thing – but what about a cuddle? Is that allowed too?

Roger Stainton
Buntingford, Hertfordshire

SIR – For the first time in over a year I hope to visit my town centre for shopping. If anyone attempts to hug me, they will be forcibly and violently resisted.

Ron Alder
Ipswich

SIR – As the whiff of garlic is thought to encourage social distancing, perhaps this pungent little vegetable should be made available on NHS prescriptions.

Ted Shorter
Tonbridge, Kent

SIR – If we are to be lumbered with Test and Trace, surely our world-beating IT sector could adapt the app for better uses.

It would be especially helpful to be pinged if one came into contact with anyone particularly boring in the pub or at a drinks party, allowing one to take appropriate isolation measures.

J. S. F. Cash
Swinford, Leicestershire

Front of the vaccine queue

SIR – Is it too late to change my surname so I get my jab earlier? Anthony Aardvark has a certain ring about it.

Tony Ounsworth
Wendover, Buckinghamshire

SIR – When I went for my vaccine I was asked if I was pregnant. I'm 76.

Diana Hitchcock
Alton, Hampshire

SIR – If the minimum age for drinking was raised to 65, pubs could safely reopen to a brisk trade from the vaccinated silver surfers.

Dave Barratt
Pitstone, Buckinghamshire

SIR – At least all these vaccines take the difficulty of working out how old potential partners are. Just ask them when they had their first jab and it all becomes clear.

Lady Lampl
Helston, Cornwall

SIR – Following a second vaccination at Epsom Racecourse, I was able to complete six furlongs.

Harry Storey
Cobham, Surrey

SIR – Within minutes of producing a vaccine passport someone will forge it. I would, like my dogs, be happy to be microchipped.

> **J. P.**
> Via email

SIR – Rewards for vaccines are not a new idea. My dog has always been given a biscuit by the vet each time he goes for his.

> **Graeme Williams**
> Kings Hill, Kent

They're what everyone's wearing these days

SIR – Assuming that masks will continue to be a part of the dress code for some while, I fear we, with other countries, will become a nation of Prince Charles ears.

> **John Bainbridge**
> Cranleigh, Surrey

SIR – Being a glass-half-full sort of person, I have already begun contemplating how we might appropriately enjoy ourselves when we are eventually released.

Might we for instance see a renaissance of the masked ball?

> **Neil Stuart**
> Plymouth, Devon

SIR – In my childhood comics only highwaymen and bank robbers wore face masks. Now such apparel is haute couture. Consequently, it is difficult to recognise one's friends, which causes problems in social intercourse. If the Covid rules are not scrapped I suggest the next edition of *Debrett's* must include guidance on relevant etiquette for modern ladies and gentlemen. It is all so frightfully tiresome for a chap.

John Pritchard
Ingatestone, Essex

SIR – Say what you like about face masks, they've saved a lot on lipstick purchases during the past year.

Jo Rogers
Stoke-on-Trent, Staffordshire

SIR – Sometimes we arrive at the shops having forgotten to bring a mask. It is reassuring that there is always a spare one to hand, on the pavement.

David Porter
Plymouth, Devon

SIR – I walked to the high street for some shopping. It was very cold and windy.

Not only did my mask protect me from the virus, it had the added bonus of keeping my nose warm.

Linda Major
London SW15

SIR – Seeing all the racegoers at Royal Ascot having a high old time, with little sign of the social distancing and mask wearing forced upon us "little people", it seems glaringly obvious that a sure-fire protection against catching or spreading Covid is a silk top hat.

T. W. Wood
Wivenhoe, Essex

SIR – I have the solution to the face mask dilemma. They should be compulsory for all government ministers, officials and members of Sage. Everyone else can stop wearing them.

Rev Philip Foster
Hemingford Abbots, Huntingdonshire

Pull those socks up

SIR – The photo accompanying your story about Jan Leeming's idea for a TV show included a fellow dressed in a smart grey suit and formal shoes but no socks. I had hoped that "mankles" was a trend that would disappear, but it seems that there are still some men who think it makes them look good. It does not. Even if you are Italian. Please go back to wearing socks, if only for the sake of the hosiery industry.

Joseph Kerrigan
London W13

SIR – One benefit from lockdown is that I
can continue to wear my Christmas socks with
impunity.

Dr Robert Seaman
Henlow, Bedfordshire

SIR – Can anyone explain why shoelaces (remember
them?) come undone at the most inappropriate
moments and yet get themselves into a more
complicated knot when you try to untie them at the
end of the day?

Carey Waite
Chailey Green, East Sussex

Top of the class

SIR – Judy Murray, who disapproves of non-
competitive school sports days, should watch the
fathers' race.

Mark Solon
London E1

SIR – Your coverage of the report suggesting pupils
should be taught magic brought back fond memories
of the Head of Biology at our school. He was a member
of the Magic Circle and, I am sure, the only member
to pull tricks out of the rabbit.

Andrew Gould
Bradfield, Devon

SIR – Some of the finest academic minds in the country believe the statue of Cecil Rhodes should be made to face the wall. What next, six of the best? Detention? Straight to bed, no supper?

Joseph Kennils
Little Wigborough, Essex

SIR – Dons are merely grown-up students from an earlier period. Oxford's seem to have omitted the "growing up" part.

Phil Collins
Tewkesbury, Gloucestershire

This could run and run

SIR – My late uncle wore an artificial left leg for most of his life. After his death my aunt sold up and returned to Bolton. She left the leg, or legs, in the roof cavity. I often wonder what became of the hoard.

John A. Turner
Bolton, Lancashire

SIR – A colour advertisement for an exercise machine in the Saturday colour supplement of a very well-known national newspaper showed that the model (young, female) had three legs. I consider that this is an extremely powerful argument against purchasing such a machine, as I can conceive of no eventuality

other than on the Isle of Man where the additional
appendage might confer an advantage.

Philip Barry
Dover, Kent

The great outdoors

SIR – Barbecues...a delightful way of ruining perfectly
good food.

Alan Anning
Sandhurst, Berkshire

SIR – Another reminder this evening of just how
much times have changed.

My next-door neighbour's son called and very
politely asked if he could recover his drone, which he
had inadvertently landed in my back garden.

Bit of a change from "Hey mister! Chuck us me ball
back!"

Alan Mottram
Tarporley, Cheshire

SIR – Until now, at this time of year, I would proceed
to the garden full of resolve, rolling up my shirtsleeves
ready to do the necessary work.

I no longer do this. Instead, I have cut the sleeves
off my gardening shirts.

Tim Snelgar
Newbury, Berkshire

SIR – Gardeners prefer to hand-wash dishes. It is an easy way to remove the soil from underneath your fingernails.

Melvyn Owen
St Ives, Cambridgeshire

SIR – Highlight of my day today was getting an email from Keith Weed, the president of the Royal Horticultural Society.

Monica Cornforth
London W5

SIR – Now that the weather is warmer I've decided it's time to grow runner beans. I always start them off in small containers made from strips of *The Daily Telegraph* newspaper.

It was particularly satisfying to tear strips from the pages showing the photos of Dominic Cummings.

He will now be doing something useful and in a week or two he can be buried in my garden.

Susan Firth
Stratford-upon-Avon, Warwickshire

SIR – Though we had a wet late winter, gardens in southern England are now parched, with no sign of rain to come. Is it already time for the water companies to make their annual threat of a hosepipe ban? That normally does the trick.

W. Stuart Hall
Mickleton, Gloucestershire

In the garden of Eden

SIR – Your article titled "Amazon advert claims tent is so easy to assemble that even women can do it" made me laugh out loud.

We all know that we invariably have to come to the aid of struggling men, but are clever enough for them not to know it.

Sue Beale
Maidenhead, Berkshire

SIR – I wish my husband could remember the "safe place" where he put the awning from our back garden last autumn.

Lynn Withey
Swindon, Wiltshire

SIR – I advised my wife of Monty Don's view that a neatly tended lawn is a symbol of male control and volunteered to abandon the weekly cut. However, she has overruled me.

Andrew Griffee
Stanford Bridge, Worcestershire

SIR – I'm pretty certain that, post-Freud, most of us know why certain people feel the need to sit astride big mowers. Nothing to do with lawns.

I've not mown my lawn yet.

Oliver Tyson
Ashby de la Zouch, Leicestershire

Weathering the changes

SIR – I had hitherto felt that the cracks in our front garden wall were due to shoddy workmanship, old age and a car reversing into it. Thanks to English Heritage I now have the insight that they are, in fact, due to climate change. I would like to extend my gratitude for this revelation.

Simon Hubbard
Brownhills, Staffordshire

SIR – I have a few trees in my garden, so I have allowed it to transition into a natural woodland glade. It is now full of empty beer cans, discarded fast food packaging, the occasional spare tyre and some plastic dog poo bags hanging from convenient branches.

Malcolm Allen
Berkhamsted, Hertfordshire

SIR – About 12 years ago I was advised to replant my garden with drought-resistant plants as only they would survive due to climate change.

They were washed away a short time later.

Steve Cattell
Grantham, Lincolnshire

SIR – I've heard that air pollution can be damaging to my health, so I've decided to stop breathing while out of the house.

Antony Thomas
Esher, Surrey

There may be trouble ahead

SIR – Today the BBC weather app said there would be thunderstorms, lightning and heavy rain.

It was actually quite a nice day – mostly sunny, some light cloud and no rain or thunderstorms at all.

Is the Met Office now being run by Professor Neil Ferguson?

David Mason
Witney, Oxfordshire

SIR – In the middle of lockdown and at the end, we hope, of the Arctic weather, our moods were lifted this morning when an ice cream van drove along the road playing "The sun has got its hat on".

That's the spirit, keep it up.

Michael Baker
Poole, Dorset

SIR – In view of my past experience, I think that weather forecasters should start their forecasts with the phrase "At a guess".

R. Tucker
Harrow, Middlesex

SIR – Your article offers: "Footwear. The nine shoes you need this summer". Please, knowing the British climate – where are my wellies?

Wyllan M. Horsfall
Sheffield, South Yorkshire

SIR – During the recent warm spell I have discovered an aid for sleeping through the high night temperatures.

The opposite of a hot water bottle, a frozen wine cooler jacket does the trick.

So far, it has been minus the bottle.

Susan Firth
Stratford-upon-Avon, Warwickshire

Nature on your doorstep

SIR – I enjoyed your article about the needs of various animals to enjoy their own space, away from humans.

Perhaps you could talk to the squirrels, some five feet away from my kitchen door, who nick the seeds and nuts from my bird feeders.

Richard Bruce
Wadhurst, East Sussex

SIR – Our fox chews the laces of my walking boots when I leave them on the porch. Has the urban fox developed to such a degree that it now knows how to floss?

Tony Parrack
London SW20

SIR – Frogs are mating early this year. Perhaps they have been locked down for too long.

Michael Groom
Teffont Evias, Wiltshire

SIR – If anyone is looking for their racing pigeons, I've had about 20 here this week eating all the niger and sunflower seeds I'd left out for the goldfinches.

They are now sitting by the pool. I might start charging.

Harriet James
Hungerford, Berkshire

Cat-a-waul

SIR – My mother had a dreadful singing voice. Whenever she began to sing our cat would jump up onto her knee and start to claw her throat.

Marion Dean
Altrincham, Cheshire

SIR – My wife, after loading boxes of dry kitten food onto the supermarket checkout belt, is frequently asked whether we have a cattery. We don't have one solitary kitten – but an abundance of happy, portly hedgehogs who refuse to hibernate.

Keith Darbyshire
Dorchester

SIR – When my husband took our cat to be neutered, he was alarmed to hear the receptionist read the diary entry. "Mr Grimes (Digby), castrate." He deposited the cat and fled.

Rosalind Grimes
Honiton, Devon

SIR – Scientists have discovered that a combination of high-protein food and being played with for 10 minutes every day can help prevent cats from bringing home dead offerings. Please can they now come up with a way for owners to stop them from using their neighbours' gardens as middens?

Charles Smith-Jones
Landrake, Cornwall

SIR – When my wife was growing up, she had a cat called Charlie. After we married, we acquired a cat and I suggested that we called him Charles II. My wife said she wanted something completely different, hence he was named Monty Python.

Chris King
Woking, Surrey

It's a dog's life

SIR – When moving into a new district my Jack
Russell made himself unpopular by showing that there
were two sorts of cats: the quick and the dead. If they
weren't one, they were soon the other. Having sorted
that out he lived in a state of armed neutrality with
what was left.

Graham Glasse
Lavenham, Suffolk

SIR – How I wish I'd waited to buy one of Boston
Dynamics' robotic dogs instead of the real puppy dog
I bought during lockdown.

The four-legged robot is self-charging – no need
for endless bowls of mince and kibble – comes when
called, does tasks with its arms instead of digging holes
in my lawn and presumably doesn't require doggy
doo-doo bags and trips to the doggy poo bin.

It is definitely designed to make the real thing
obsolescent.

Angela Lawrence
Woodbridge, Suffolk

SIR – True to the intelligence of his breed, our
spaniel, Bracken, must have foreseen the national
pet food shortage. Is it now time to forgive the treats
buried in our borders and the crusts under the sofa?

David and Sandra Morris
Moreton in Marsh, Gloucestershire

SIR – As a new owner of a pedigree parti poodle, I have learnt that:

Dogs sleep 18 hours a day (but this excludes 11pm to 2am).

Dogs eat at least two meals a day (even with a "slow eating" bowl, this takes under 2 minutes).

Dogs go loopy or "get the zoomies" for at least 15 minutes a day.

Dogs chew for at least an hour a day (10 minutes on dog toys, the rest on plastic or rubber domestic items or shoes).

Dogs like around 2 hours of walks per day (with 30 minutes actually in the direction the owner is going).

The rest of the time, they just waste.

Mark Hodson
Bristol

SIR – I notice admission guidelines often include "children and well-behaved dogs". In my experience, it should be "dogs and well-behaved children".

Justice Hawkins
Great Torrington, Devon

SIR – I get annoyed when the owner assures me that the dog is only being friendly as it attempts to lick my private parts.

John Challiss
Bisley, Surrey

SIR – A ploy I have found effective when a thoughtless human allows their pooch to come too close to my dogs (who prefer their space not to be invaded) is to smile generously, and perhaps a little manically, when told, "He is only being friendly".

I then open my arms and walk towards them, quoting Piero's words from *The Revenger's Tragedy* by Middleton and/or Tourneur.

"Oh come, let me hug your bosoms."

If they protest before beating a hasty retreat... "I am only being friendly!"

This has worked well and ensures I and my dogs are given a wide berth.

Margaret Ellis
Ingleton, North Yorkshire

SIR – My dog prefers to be on the lead. She then doesn't have to worry that I might have run off somewhere and she can tow me the way she wants to go knowing that I must follow.

Graham Nowell
Clifton Hampden, Oxfordshire

One man's trash

SIR – I am a member of a group of local litter pickers, the Coggeshall Litterati, which does its best to keep the rising tide of litter at bay from our local roads and public footpaths. Our haul comprises a depressingly monotonous sequence of takeaway wrappers, plastic drinks bottles and coffee cups.

Perhaps this is why we and our fellow litter-picking addicts from neighbouring Earls Colne get inordinately excited when something different turns up. For the discovery of ditch-bound shoes, always singly and never in pairs, a couple of us have developed a shoe dance similar to the gold dance enacted by metal detectorists on the discovery of gold.

However, my friend from Earls Colne was at a loss for a suitable reaction to the discovery of an outsized rubber model, with an impressive level of detail, of a distinctly male part of the anatomy, which she retrieved from the road which joins our two villages. It is obvious how takeaway wrappers end up on the roadside; but how do people not notice they have lost a shoe or a rubber penis?

Tina Sivyer
Coggeshall, Essex

SIR – At home in Staffordshire, the rural lane which runs past our 19th-century farmworker's cottage is frequently festooned with fast food detritus. How refreshing, then, to be holidaying in the Cotswolds where, on a walk to the local farm shop, we came upon an abandoned box of Veuve Clicquot on the verge.

Michael Pearson
Tatenhill Common, Staffordshire

SIR – Do discarded face masks now outnumber elastic bands dropped by postmen?

Mark Solon
London E1

SIR – Surely the finest example of a successful
litter pick is recorded in the King James Bible.
St Mark's Gospel records that having fed "about five
thousand" with "five loaves and the two fishes", the
Christ's disciples collected "twelve baskets full of
the fragments".

That's what I would call a result!

C. D. Henderson
Cranleigh, Surrey

The importance of being idle

SIR – Following the announcement in today's *Telegraph*
of the formation of The Boredom Society, I am
pleased to announce the establishment of The Apathy
Society, and to declare myself its first non-member.

Peter Ball
Hilton, Derbyshire

Hair is the news

SIR – The Chancellor should consider introducing a
beard tax in his forthcoming Budget.

Judging by the proliferation of beards all around
us, the national debt would benefit greatly.

Bob Wilson
Wolverhampton, Staffordshire

A YEAR IN
POLITICS

Governed by the head

SIR — One of the unforeseen consequences of Donald Trump losing the presidential election is that on 20 January 2021 our very own Boris Johnson became the world leader with the most ridiculous hairstyle.

May I take this opportunity to offer my sincere congratulations to the Prime Minister.

Richard Holloway
Nailsea, North Somerset

SIR — If Boris Johnson would like to keep his hair under control, might I suggest a light touch of Brylcreem until the barber's chair is available? Failing that, never stand near a Van de Graaff generator.

Don Fitzroy Smith
Chester

SIR — I am hoping that once Boris Johnson's dad trips over his hair then hairdressers will be allowed to reopen.

Joan Manning
Barton on Sea, Hampshire

SIR — It appears that our Prime Minister has taken early advantage of the easing of tonsorial restrictions. However, it does seem that he might have been urgently recalled mid-cut, causing the barber's full intentions to be cut short.

Lovat Timbrell
Brighton, East Sussex

Parental guidance

SIR – It is disconcerting that Angela Merkel is known in Germany as "*Mutti*". Can one imagine the British calling Boris "Daddy"? On second thoughts, there are quite a number who probably could.

Peter Wellby
Chiddingly, East Sussex

SIR – I suggest that Father Christmas drops a watch down the chimney at No 10, thereby allowing the Prime Minister to arrive on time for his Downing Street briefings.

Claire McCombie
Woodbridge, Suffolk

SIR – We have a leak sensor in our house which gives us a warning should a leak be detected. Perhaps No 10 Downing Street should get one installed.

Mike Jenkins
Waterlooville, Hampshire

SIR – How cheering to see an image of Larry the cat, marking his ten years in Downing Street. But your caption writer has erred in stating he has "worked" under three prime ministers. Cats may occasionally do something useful or entertaining if it suits them, but they certainly do not "work".

Dr Hilary Aitken
Kilmacolm, Renfrewshire

There's no accounting for taste

SIR – I fear that Boris Johnson may be suffering from so-called "long Covid".

From what we have learnt of his recent domestic redecorations, he appears to have yet to recover his sense of taste.

James D. C. Perks
Bicester, Oxfordshire

SIR – I suppose the next time Boris and Carrie are reported shouting at one another in their flat, they may simply be trying to make themselves heard over the soft furnishings.

Richard Thorns
Crowborough, East Sussex

SIR – Having just seen a quote for the refurbishment of my son's London house, I think Boris Johnson has got a bargain.

Valerie Arends
London SW6

SIR – I am amazed that the Prime Minister has time to even consider redecorating his apartment.

I have been retired for 19 years and still haven't started on the lounge.

Martin Seligman
Reading

SIR – Television news commentary on governance of the country seems to be moving from questions over choice of wallpaper to payments for the PM's home child support.

I don't imagine this is what Thatcher had in mind when she warned us about "the nanny state".

Robert Barlow
Little Bookham, Surrey

In sickness and in health

SIR – I wish the Prime Minister had held his wedding after 21 June. He could have held a reception at London's Nightingale Hospital. The hospital would finally have had some use.

Mark Macauley
Warminster, Wiltshire

SIR – It's good to see that Carrie has finally made an honest man of her other half.

Paul Bendit
Arlington, East Sussex

SIR – Was Dilyn a bridesmaid?

Kate Graeme-Cook
Brixham, Devon

U-turn and turn again

SIR – Given the ongoing farrago of indecision,
U-turns and appalling PR from this Government,
I find myself wistfully dreaming of a previous prime
minister whose faults were merely those of potentially
breaking up the UK, diluting tertiary education and
not being totally honest regarding Iraq.

Andrew Main
Shaftesbury, Dorset

SIR – Back in the 1960s I bought a greetings card that
bore the inscription: "I used to be indecisive, but now
I'm not so sure."

Would that I still had it – Boris Johnson could have
deployed it as a campaign banner.

Dr John Gladstone
Gerrards Cross, Buckinghamshire

SIR – Many, many years ago when I was a Sandhurst
cadet, a Company Sergeant Major Instructor shouted
(expletives excluded!) to a hesitant cadet: "Lead your
men, Sir. I don't care where you lead them, but lead
them somewhere!" It is a pity that the Prime Minister
and senior members of the Cabinet did not receive
such leadership training.

David Walters
Corbridge, Northumberland

SIR – I understand that the political gymnast Boris Johnson, who recently transitioned from being a Conservative to self-identifying as a socialist, is being allowed to perform as a Tory.

This is grossly unfair to real Conservatives who may feel that they are discriminated against.

Paul Jones
Nottingham

SIR – Could someone please form a Conservative Party so that I can use my vote at the next election?

Peter Flesher
Halifax, West Yorkshire

SIR – Does anyone know how many nails are needed to complete a coffin? The Government is trying so hard to get the job over and done with.

Olly Plater
Holmer Green, Buckinghamshire

SIR – I read today there is a Chairman of the Common Sense Group of Conservative MPs. I wonder what on earth they discuss.

S. M.
Via email

SIR – I didn't expect that handwriting my letter cancelling my membership of the Conservative Party would give me so much satisfaction.

Barbara Smith
Stafford

SIR – Might I advise Boris Johnson that if he wishes to keep the Union together then the last thing he should do is visit Scotland.

Mike McKone
Kirkby Stephen, Cumbria

A Cabinet of horrors

SIR – I see that we shall shortly have to produce a valid reason should we wish to leave the country. Would "Priti Patel" suffice?

Roger Little
Tisbury, Wiltshire

SIR – Surely there are more intelligent and able fireplace salespersons who would make a far better Education Secretary than the present incumbent.

A. Lloyd
Liverpool

SIR – You report that "animals with a backbone" will have their feelings recognised legally in order to raise welfare standards.

I believe this shows a lack of compassion for our politicians of late.

Simon Crowley
Kemsing, Kent

SIR – I have come to the conclusion that our country is run by a group of headless chickens with jerky knees.

> **Ernie Warner**
> Faversham, Kent

SIR – What is "honourable" about an MP or "right" about some of them?

> **Barrie Crave**
> Kirk Ella, East Yorkshire

SIR – I note the proposal that ministers and senior officials be prevented from lobbying for five years after leaving office. I would add the monastic vows of silence, obedience and chastity, in some cases while still in office.

> **A. Eastwood**
> Bromley, Kent

SIR – Wouldn't it make sense to appoint public officials who are up to the job rather than those that still need to learn lessons?

> **Tony King**
> Hove, East Sussex

SIR – Why is it that the media so often refer to "the high standards we expect from our politicians"?
  I for one expect nothing but the most miserable standards from them and am seldom disappointed.

> **Andrew Swanston**
> Horsell, Surrey

SIR – Successive governments went disastrously wrong when the fools stopped listening to London cabbies.

Lance Warrington
Northleach, Gloucestershire

Cummings must go

SIR – We do not need people like the underdressed Dominic Cummings in this country.
  Send him to Russia.

N. S.
Via email

SIR – I am surprised that Dominic Cummings can be bothered with our little country full of people who are so clearly inferior to him. He deserves his own country where every citizen has the inestimable advantage of being Dominic Cummings and nobody will challenge his ideas. What a pity that "Dominican Republic" is already in use.

Jolyon Cox
Witney, Oxfordshire

SIR – During my time in the Royal Navy we had plenty of words for the likes of Dominic Cummings. Alas, none are printable in *The Daily Telegraph*.

Eddie Lodge
Plymouth, Devon

SIR – Boris has clearly failed to heed the advice about the location of once-trusted cronies with respect to the tent.

> **Bill Galvin**
> Stockport, Cheshire

SIR – Anyone who thinks the British people are gullible enough to believe that Barnard Castle is an eye test centre has got to be a little untrustworthy.

> **Nairn Lawson**
> Portbury, Somerset

SIR – Mr Cummings will get his comeuppance in the end; sneaks always do. At school, they'd be popped into the holly bush in the quad. That cured them.

> **Julien Chilcott-Monk**
> Winchester, Hampshire

SIR – What chance for weirdos and misfits now?

> **Malcolm Greenhill**
> St Leonards-on-Sea, East Sussex

SIR – As we no longer have capital punishment for even the most heinous of crimes, I think I have come up with an effective replacement for what was often referred to as the "ultimate deterrent".

Incarcerate those found guilty of serious crimes at a remote location with only Dominic Cummings and Martin Bashir for company.

> **Robert Readman**
> West Bournemouth, Dorset

SIR – Let's face it. He even looks like a sour grape.

J. Walker
Barnstaple, Devon

SIR – Perhaps now is the perfect time for Dominic Cummings to apply for the job as political adviser to Prince Harry and emigrate.

Dr Malcolm Gamble
Southwell, Nottinghamshire

What Bercow did next

SIR – I see John Bercow is joining the Labour Party. It is indeed rare to see a rat actually join a sinking ship.

Peter Little
Herne Bay, Kent

SIR – Today I witnessed a bear heading for some woods carrying a loo roll.

Wiliam McWilliams
Ashford, Kent

SIR – A local business hereabouts displays the sign "Everybody brings joy to this establishment: some when they arrive, some when they leave."

I expect the Tory Party will recognise the feeling.

Nicholas Franks
Dorchester

SIR — I have just heard on the radio a commentator describing John Bercow as a Marmite figure. I think such a statement is wholly unfair. Millions of people really like Marmite.

Mick Ferrie
Mawnan Smith, Cornwall

Hancock's half-hour is up

SIR — Those whom the gods would destroy they first made mad.

Please ask Matt Hancock to take out a few minutes from his lunacy to read Euripides.

Dr Maxim Segal
London N3

SIR — It is reported that the Queen told the PM, at his weekly audience with her, that Matt Hancock "was full of..." and that he interjected with "full of beans".

It was unmannerly of him to interrupt: if Her Majesty wishes to use the "s" word then that is her prerogative.

Kenneth Preston
Hillsborough, Co Down

SIR — Sherelle Jacobs reckons Boris has "a Hancock-shaped headache". So do I. The difference is that I am married to mine.

Sandra Hancock
Exeter, Devon

SIR – Well I'll say this much, having spotted him on telly going for a run.

Matt Hancock has got terrific legs.

Edward Thomas
Eastbourne, East Sussex

SIR – Through thick and thin throughout the pandemic my husband has never wavered in his dislike or criticism of Matt Hancock. Not one appearance or announcement has changed his view.

He has been proved correct. How irritating.

Marguerite Beard-Gould
Walmer, Kent

SIR – Fortunately for Matt Hancock, his boss can fully empathise over his alleged affair with Gina Coladangelo. I wonder if this type of extramarital activity might even be included in a minister's job description.

Christopher Learmont-Hughes
Caldy, Wirral

SIR – The Government's new message on Covid (as demonstrated by Matt Hancock): "hands to bums, face to face, tums to tums".

Colin Belcher
Gloucester

SIR – If I was to go around squeezing the bottoms of all those I love, I'm sure I'd be arrested – and not just for breaking social distancing rules.

Joanna Bunkham
Swansea

SIR – Can we hope that "breaking the social distancing rules" will enter the lexicon as a new euphemism for an extramarital affair?

E. J. Barraclough
Ipswich

SIR – I think it would be a good idea to present any male going to work at No 10 with a pair of braces.
It might help them to keep their trousers up.

Barrie Schofield
Huddersfield, West Yorkshire

SIR – Sarah Vine, the wife of Michael Gove, suggests that government ministers are attractive to other women because of their "brilliance".
Were they that brilliant they would not be caught in the first place.

John Hutton
Worksop, Nottinghamshire

SIR – I have had my doubts about Mr Hancock's judgement for some time. Any man who insists on wearing the same overlong, bland, pink tie every day for 15 months has flawed wisdom.

Benjamin L. C. Smith
Hedge End, Hampshire

SIR – Am I alone in my growing desire to take Matt Hancock behind the metaphorical bike sheds and beat some sense into him? He has now entirely lost the plot and I, for one, have entirely lost my patience.

Will Curtis
Bures, Suffolk

SIR – If Matt Hancock was my son-in-law, he would get a sound thrashing. I am from Glasgow. He would not get up.

John M. Scott
Aspley Guise, Bedfordshire

SIR – I think it is very important to track down the individual, or group of people, who leaked the security footage of Hancock's affair to the press.

It is a vital prerequisite for giving the leaker a knighthood for their services.

Robert Peck
Heslington, North Yorkshire

SIR – When I heard that a government scandal was about to break, I excitedly hoped that Professor Chris Whitty had been caught with his slides down.

David Wiltshire
Bedford

SIR – Perhaps the Government can now get on with governing, without distractions.

John Gander
Worthing, West Sussex

SIR – What a pity that Mr Hancock wasn't discovered months ago. We might have had Sajid Javid instead and been released in the early summer.

Stan Grabecki
St Albans, Hertfordshire

As opposed to what?

SIR – It has often been said that to be a good government there needs to be a strong opposition.

Sir Keir Starmer is doing such a poor job that the Conservatives are currently having to fill both roles.

Alan Croft
Cambridge

SIR – If Sir Keir Starmer had been Prime Minister in 1940 at the time of the Dunkirk evacuation he would probably have insisted that all the little ships had been registered and complied with safety regulations before they took part in the emergency.

John Sharp
Great Glen, Leicestershire

SIR – Sir Keir Starmer explained his party's lack of success in Hartlepool – and accepted his responsibility for it – dressed in a business suit, wearing a bland tie and standing in front of shelves laden with legal tomes.

And he wonders why the local voters regard him as an alien.

Richard R. Dolphin
Taunton, Somerset

SIR – Sir Keir Starmer should note that his merely not being Jeremy Corbyn is not enough.

Bruce Denness
Niton, Isle of Wight

SIR – After Labour's dismal performance in the local elections, it is clear that the name Momentum is not only no longer appropriate but may well be a breach of the Trade Descriptions Act.

Paul Jones
Nottingham

SIR – The result in the Batley and Spen by-election can only be described as a humiliating victory for Labour.

> **Julian Hales**
> Saffron Walden, Essex

SIR – We have witnessed the birth of a new verb: to starm, meaning to see a great victory in what is really no more than a narrow escape. Someone who does this is, by extension, a starmer.

> **Glenn Mitchell**
> London SW16

SIR – If Angela Rayner is the answer, then it must have been a very stupid question.

> **G. W. Swift**
> Newcastle-under-Lyme, Staffordshire

SIR – Hurrah. What a boost for the Conservatives. Diane Abbott has resurfaced.

> **John Dorricott**
> Barton on Sea, Hampshire

SIR – When will all the ex-prime ministers realise that there is nothing more ex than an ex?

> **Martin Wood**
> Malmesbury, Wiltshire

Lib Dems break the blue wall

SIR – Seeing that the pseudo-Lib Dems and Greens are apparently running the country at the moment, perhaps the electorate of Chesham thought they might just as well vote for the real thing.

Keith Chambers
Brockenhurst, Hampshire

SIR – It is always a surprise when the Liberal Democrats are victorious in anything. It is never a surprise that once having tasted a victory they go on and on and on about it.

Stefan Badham
Portsmouth, Hampshire

Locked down and fed up

SIR – With the lifting of restrictions deferred yet again, will the practice of banging pans etc. to support the NHS be superseded by booing the Government at 6pm each day?

John Pickles
St Peter Port, Guernsey

SIR – The proposed tortuously slow escape from lockdown could only have been devised by people with bullet-proof salaries and gold-plated pension schemes, advised by people with bullet-proof salaries, gold-plated pension schemes and job security.

> **Tony Rigby**
> Middleton-on-Sea, West Sussex

SIR – If we are to have our basic freedoms suspended until any government can run the NHS efficiently, we are in for a very bleak time.

> **Robin Cantellow**
> Ashbourne, Derbyshire

SIR – Small wonder that the Government does not support creating a specific offence of non-fatal strangulation. After all, that is exactly what it is doing with repeated lockdown–release cycles.

> **David Proctor**
> Pickering, North Yorkshire

SIR – If things keep going the way they are, we shall reach herd mentality before herd immunity. Definitely not what the human race needs.

> **Christopher Hunt**
> Swanley, Kent

SIR – Apparently the way to protest against the restrictions on peaceful protesting is to riot.

> **Tim Nixon**
> Braunton, Devon

SIR – My dream is clear, concise, consistent and confident messaging on Covid from the Government. Sadly, I awake still confused.

James Service
Ludlow, Shropshire

SIR – The Isle of Man's chief minister is reported as saying, "We beat the virus once and we have done so again." That's a bit like saying, "Giving up smoking is easy – I've done it dozens of times."

Peter Harper
Salisbury, Wiltshire

SIR – In a Parliamentary debate on the plight of hedgehogs, Matt Vickers (Con., Stockton South) ridiculed a 2015 suggestion that the hedgehog should be adopted as Britain's national animal on the grounds that an animal that rolls into a ball at the first sign of danger and sleeps for half a year would not necessarily portray the image we want as a nation.

Given the behaviour of a large proportion of the public, scientists, organisations and politicians over the last year or so of the pandemic, it now seems quite appropriate.

Peter Knowles
Leigh-on-Sea, Essex

It's a date

SIR – Lockdown has eased but still has a sting in its tail. I see with horror that the "Glorious Twelfth" now refers to 12 April.

Antony Mackenzie-Smith
Abergavenny, Monmouthshire

SIR – I am uncertain about the proposed National Day of Reflection on the anniversary of the first lockdown. By 23 March we will have had a whole year of reflection already.

Fiona Wild
Cheltenham, Gloucestershire

SIR – For the past 18 months I have regularly reassured my granddaughter that restrictions/ regulations would be short-lived and lifted in three weeks, three months, in time for Christmas, by Easter and definitely on 21 June.

Sadly she no longer believes a word I say.

Brian Ross
Bradford, West Yorkshire

SIR – "One last heave," says the Prime Minister. At least he acknowledges that his policy makes us sick.

Cynthia Harrod-Eagles
Northwood, Middlesex

Recollections may vary

SIR – Now that the number of deaths has exceeded 100,000, another pandemic has broken out. The latest variant is called hindsight and is spreading virulently among experts and politicians. The symptoms include acute knowledge of what the Government should have done.

James Johnstone
Westerham, Kent

SIR – With NASA now beginning to come down on the side that UFOs may indeed be real, surely it won't be long before the scientists are telling us we must not relax in the face of a possible Mars variant of Covid.

Philip Hall
Petersfield, Hampshire

Road to nowhere

SIR – The real problem with any "road map" out of lockdown is that the vast majority of the population will struggle to follow the directions.
 I blame Sat Nav.

Mark Shaw
Heathfield, East Sussex

SIR – Now that Covid deaths are well below the average daily deaths from traffic accidents, will the Government follow the data, lift the lockdown and close the roads?

Malcolm Symonds
Ashtead, Surrey

SIR – The Prime Minister referred to 19 July as a "terminus". I find this troubling; the terminus is the point where a train driver relocates to the other end of the train to take it back in the opposite direction.

Will we ever be free again?

Thomas Howey
Buckhurst Hill, Essex

Tested to the limit

SIR – The Government's Covid-19 email bulletin service has kindly sent me 44 documents yesterday and 75 today. I am trying to keep up. I hope they will not be asking questions afterwards.

Graham Clifton
Kingston-upon-Thames, Surrey

SIR – There is much talk of the lessons to be learnt from the pandemic. One might be that there seem to be an awful lot of professors in this country. Another is that few of them seem to have a clue what they are talking about.

William Martin
Chinnor, Oxfordshire

Following the scientists

SIR – I have noted the similarities between relying on scientists today and the augurs of ancient Rome and wondered if they changed the chicken's diet to obtain a different result.

Simon Longe
Beccles, Suffolk

SIR – An acronym like Sage would imply wisdom and truth. It seems neither is the case.

Rena Guttridge
Ripponden, West Yorkshire

SIR – It's clear that Sage needs a rebrand.
From the data available to me, I suggest:

Conservative-
Loathing
Unelected
Electorate-
Lecturing
Evidence-
Suppressing
Schemers

Andrew Adamson
Chichester, West Sussex

SIR – If the current Sage group are looking for a suitable motto, may I suggest:

Things will get much worse before they get worse.

John Scott
Birstall, Leicestershire

SIR – It is becoming increasingly obvious that Sage is an accurate acronym: Scientists Against General Enjoyment.

Richard W. Turner
Nazeing, Essex

SIR – I was intrigued by Monty Don's weekend tips on Friday's *Gardeners' World* – cut back the sage. I wonder if the Prime Minister was watching?

Peter Hill
Teddington, Middlesex

SIR – I do wish that all these scientists would leave the modelling to Airfix or to Naomi Campbell. Both are much better at it.

M. Burbidge
Bexhill-on-Sea, East Sussex

SIR – In our introduction to psychiatry at medical school in the 1980s, we were taught the adage that neurotics build castles in the air and psychotics live in them while psychiatrists collect the rent. In the madness of lockdown I would suggest that the epidemiological modellers built the castle and that certain members of Sage have resided there in close company with the Health Secretary. There is no rent to collect because business is on hold. Unless the

Prime Minister and First Ministers raise the portcullis and lower the drawbridge, the lunatics will continue to run the asylum.

David Scott-Coombes MS FRCS
Llysworney, Glamorgan

Off to see the wizard

SIR – Professor Chris Whitty, the Government's chief medical adviser, has gained celebrity status by regularly appearing on our screens offering doom and gloom scenarios while looking like a tortoise emerging from its shell.

Maybe he picked up someone else's jacket after a drunken advisory meeting and was too embarrassed to admit his mistake, or it was bought for him in the hope that he'd grow into it; or maybe he has some kind of Wizard of Oz complex, appearing big and powerful, when he is really wearing a huge suit to disguise his puny shoulders.

Whatever the reason, his apparel mirrors the policy advice he gives: totally ridiculous.

Lindsay Ward
Broughton-in-Furness, Cumbria

SIR – Why aren't Professors Whitty, Ferguson et al in the Cabinet? They are after all in charge of us.

Boris Johnson can keep his job as their press officer.

Peter Gold
Ashbourne, Derbyshire

A country retreat

SIR – Glorious mid-summer heatwave, classic country house with extensive grounds and of course staff laid on. What's not to like about 10 days' self-isolation, Boris?

Bill Collier
Earby, Lancashire

SIR – I trust that the Prime Minister is having his copy of *The Daily Telegraph* pushed under his bedroom door while he is isolating. To make sure that he is getting all the advice that he needs, he merely has to read the letters pages and act accordingly.

Christopher Leach
Chalfont St Peter, Buckinghamshire

The year that wasn't

SIR – In foisting a lockdown upon the country in March 2020, the Prime Minister has, perhaps unwittingly, verified Einstein's theory of time dilation.

Three weeks in Boris Johnson's reference frame has been 15 months for the rest of us.

Brendon Swidecki
Chichester, West Sussex

SIR – Will whoever has stolen the PM's goalposts, please return them immediately.

Ken White
Princes Risborough, Buckinghamshire

SIR – It's a good thing we got Brexit done. It's very difficult to kick two cans down the road.

Keith Macpherson
Clevedon, Somerset

SIR – In my opinion, the best term to describe the PM is "a poltroon".

Diana Dixon
Tonbridge, Kent

SIR – If Boris had had to give the order to launch D-Day he would have held back because of the worrying weather reports for 6 June 1944, and today I could well be writing this letter in German.

Pamela R. Goldsack
Banstead, Surrey

SIR – I may be the only person in these freedom-loving islands who wishes Boris Johnson to stay on as Prime Minister.

After 50 years of marriage to a Yorkshire girl, this is the first time she has admitted to me that someone's utterances have left her "speechless".

Long may it continue.

David Evans
Wilmslow, Cheshire

Shot in the arm

SIR – The Pfizer vaccine was given to me by a very smart British Army sergeant in combat dress. Given the EU's latest moves, this suddenly seems more appropriate than the usual white coat.

John Jones
London SW19

SIR – It is sobering to consider that those responsible for the EU vaccine debacle are the same people who would have ultimate control over an EU army at a time of war.

David Watt
Oakley, Buckinghamshire

SIR – According to the European Statistical Office, of the 25 million Europeans who recently received the AstraZeneca vaccine, during the following week, 25 people broke their leg, 28 got divorced, 87 developed erectile dysfunction, 35 had a car accident, 987 lost their keys and 127 had diarrhoea. Therefore, after you have been vaccinated you should exercise extreme caution.

Francis Forbes
Eastbourne, East Sussex

SIR – Many question whether children should be vaccinated for Covid. Perhaps lockdowns should remain in place until all children have reached adulthood.

Nicholas Crocker
Yeovil, Somerset

SIR – Mr Johnson in his great wisdom has decided that it is house arrest rather than vaccinations which is defeating Covid. I am due for my second jab; do I keep my appointment or cower behind the sofa?

Alan Sabatini
Bournemouth, Dorset

SIR – As Mr Johnson claims that he "never felt a thing" when receiving his vaccination, does that not demonstrate that he must be unbelievably thick-skinned?

Peter H. York
Daventry, Northamptonshire

SIR – It seems the science of vaccination is beyond the grasp of our politicians and a more simple approach is needed; therefore to protect us from bird flu a chicken bone through our noses should do it.

Alan G. Morton
Wymondham, Norfolk

SIR – At the end of last year the Prime Minister announced that the cavalry, in the shape of a vaccine, was coming to our aid.

No doubt he had the heroics of the Scots Greys at Waterloo in mind; instead, his bungling and indecision is turning it more into the Light Brigade at Balaclava.

Charlie Bladon
Cattistock, Dorset

One-man army

SIR – The defence review and reduction in the Armed Forces is plainly a move in the right direction, but through timidity the principle has not been pushed to its logical conclusion. A lean, agile and tech-savvy deterrent able to fight the wars of the future, and at a cost bearable to the Treasury, will only be achieved when it comprises just one man equipped with a jet-pack, water-wings, pepper-spray and the latest smartphone.

If James Bond is not available, perhaps Eddie the Eagle could be persuaded out of retirement.

Paul Simmons
East Twickenham, Middlesex

SIR – If asked, the British Army would in all probability now not have the resources to help South Africa.

But take heart, Britons; our Forces do have some small remote-controlled aeroplanes.

Mike Scott-Hayward
Cupar, Fife

SIR – To modernise the Army all troops will now be trained to send abusive texts to the enemy (you are so nasty, I am going to tell my dad about you, you smell) and also shown how to throw their i-Phones to the most devastating effect as a last resort.

Colin Belcher
Gloucester

SIR – Air Chief Marshal Sir Mike Wigston is calling for the RAF to reach net-zero carbon emissions by 2040. Good luck, though, personally, I think the project for a solar-powered night fighter is a non-starter.

J. Alan Smith
Epping, Essex

SIR – Having spent a childhood in far-flung outposts and been on the receiving end of numerous Naval visits, I was shocked to see the rust on HMS *Queen Elizabeth* as she left Portsmouth on her maiden operational mission. Funds may be low, but surely the officers and crew could have had a whip-round and sent someone in to John Lewis for some grey paint.

John Hammond
Drummuir, Banffshire

SIR – When my long-time Army wife, Anne, read the headline, "Army to lose 10,000 soldiers over 10 years", she retorted: "Well they should be better at teaching them map reading then".

John Nelson
Amesbury, Wiltshire

Taxing times

SIR – I am not usually in the habit of drinking before the sun is over the yardarm but when I read on the front page of the *Telegraph* at seven-thirty this morning that my council tax bill "will increase by up to £100 a month", I felt compelled to pour myself a very stiff whisky.

Bruce Chalmers
Goring-by-Sea, West Sussex

The full weight of the law

SIR – I do hope the Lord Chief Justice's call for slimmed-down juries will help in the fight against obesity.

Mark Solon
London E1

SIR – Is credulity an essential qualification for membership of a parole board?

Richard Jenkins
Beaconsfield, Buckinghamshire

SIR – It's reported that there has been a 50 per cent increase in crime involving e-scooters.

Surely the police must be similarly equipped to chase the miscreants, preferably to the *Dick Barton* theme tune "Devil's Gallop".

> **Bob Stebbings**
> Chorleywood, Hertfordshire

For their eyes only

SIR – The fact that a 50-page secret Ministry of Defence dossier has been found in a soggy heap at a bus stop in Kent really is extremely serious. There is far too much litter spoiling our countryside.

> **Ron Kirby**
> Dorchester

SIR – I have a briefcase I no longer use. Should I donate it to the Ministry of Defence?

> **Mervyn Vallance**
> Maldon, Essex

I'll do the honours

SIR – How long before Dominic Cummings appears in an Honours List "for services to North-East tourism"?

> **Elaine Winter**
> Whyteleafe, Surrey

SIR – I should like to apply for
   The post of Poet Laureate because
   I too can write prose
   And break it up without
   Punctuation
   Meter or rhyme
   And call it a eulogy.

> **Robert Barlow**
> Little Bookham, Surrey

SIR – I've decided that I no longer want to be famous enough to merit a statue in my local town. Once it's revealed that I used to ping girls' bra straps when at secondary school, I fear that the "retain and explain" brigade would paint me a sexist monster, regardless of my achievements in ending war and poverty throughout the known universe.

> **Iain Findlay**
> Crewe, Cheshire

Fur flies in Holyrood

SIR – We have a pair of Jack Russells, who are the best of friends most of the time, then suddenly they have a scrap; the only way to make them separate is to throw them into a bucket of cold water.

   Surely the Scottish government could afford a slightly larger bucket for this purpose.

> **Richard Beaugie**
> Ashford, Kent

SIR – I thought Punch and Judy was traditionally an English comedy, albeit with Italian roots. Alex Salmond and Nicola Sturgeon seem to be determined to relive it as a completely Scottish tragedy.

Mark Lichfield
Blandford Forum, Dorset

SIR – Wanted: Candidates for Alex Salmond's Alba Party.

Scotsmen – or women – with a grievance preferred.

Must be proficient in axe-grinding, mud-slinging and hole-digging.

Lynette Johnson
Udny, Aberdeenshire

SIR – Nicola Sturgeon is now at the stage where she is adversely affecting my blood pressure to the same extent as Jeremy Corbyn did.

Kevin Dowling
Welbourn, Lincolnshire

SIR – Nicola Sturgeon and the SNP are turning Scotland into a banana republic, without even the benefit of bananas. With the possible exception of Fife.

Donald Montgomery
Glasgow

SIR — It is never difficult to distinguish between a Scotswoman with a minority government and a ray of sunshine.

Andrew Graham
Upper Poppleton, North Yorkshire

SIR — Nicola Sturgeon and her cohorts apparently believe that 49 per cent is a majority. That may well explain why Scottish education is now so poor.

Fiona Robertson
Dumfries

SIR — If Nicola Sturgeon is looking for a song to support her politicizing, I recommend "Anything You Can Do, I Can Do Better" from *Annie Get Your Gun*.

Jeremy Burton
Wokingham, Berkshire

SIR — Nicola Sturgeon sets aside five hours in her diary to give evidence to the committee on the Scottish government's handling of allegations against her predecessor.

Meanwhile, "No" voters across Scotland are purchasing popcorn.

Clare Gill
Birstall, West Yorkshire

Settling auld scores

SIR – To save the time and cost of an independence referendum, could we use the next football match between England and Scotland to decide the issue?

Scotland wins and gains independence. England wins and we let Scotland have independence.

> **Amanda Hume**
> Sutton Coldfield, West Midlands

SIR – I would happily support the Scots in their bid for independence so long as they promise to stop exporting bagpipes.

> **Michael Hartley**
> Kendal, Cumbria

SIR – Upgrade Hadrian's Wall.

> **Timothy Dyson**
> Eaton, Nottinghamshire

SIR – In the event of an independent Scotland, who gets the BBC? It cannot serve two masters. Perhaps Scotland could have it as a farewell present.

> **Justice Hawkins**
> Great Torrington, Devon

SIR – On a video conference much of the small talk was about Covid vaccines. After a few minutes, a colleague from Scotland made the observation that callers from England kept referring to the AstraZeneca vaccine as the "Oxford" vaccine.

"In Scotland," he reflected, "our officials never mention 'Oxford' because to do so would break our national mantra that nothing good ever came out of England."

Does the proposed Cabinet member for the Union understand the scale of their task?

Dr David Slawson
Nairn

Wake me up when it's all over

SIR — Kate Bingham and her marvellous team who developed and distributed the Covid vaccines have another task of an immediate nature. They need to develop a vaccine that will cure people of "being woke".

This needs to happen with considerable urgency; casualties are rising at an alarming rate. Among them are the National Trust, the Labour Party, the BBC and Oxford University — to name just a few.

I only wish to contribute a single idea concerning how the vaccine be administered: by a large mallet to the head. That way if the vaccine was ineffective perhaps the mallet would have knocked some sense into the recipient.

Tim Brand
Long Sutton, Lincolnshire

SIR – Apparently Roger Hallam, the founder of Extinction Rebellion, would like to see "young, sexy people" filmed being restrained and arrested by the police. This is a bit of a sad and, some may say, creepy aspiration for a 55-year-old man, but surely he could satisfy these urges in some grimy corner of the Internet instead and leave the rest of us in peace.

Jon Groocock
Glastonbury, Somerset

The end is (almost) nigh

SIR – I have just received a news article on my Microsoft News Feed telling me that, according to NASA scientists, Earth will lose its oxygen atmosphere in about a billion years.

As if this were not worrying enough, I noticed with alarm that the article itself was over a week old.

Paul Jones
Radcliffe-on-Trent, Nottinghamshire

SIR – It's absolutely unbelievable that a Rover has landed on Mars. The last one I had could hardly get out of the drive. Well done British Leyland.

Peter Fraser
Leeds, West Yorkshire

SIR – A message was sent from Mars to Earth only 11 minutes after the space probe landed. It took almost as long this morning to access BT's website to check my account.

I certainly need Perseverance.

Lesley McDowell
Herne Bay, Kent

SIR – How sad that David Bowie is not with us to celebrate the landing on Mars, and with it, the potential answer to the question that he posed to us all 50 years ago.

Nigel Lines
Ferndown, Dorset

SIR – I suggest that we find out where that meteorite came from, whether there is intelligent life there and, if so, send it back. We don't want another Elgin Marbles situation.

Graham Fish
Hertford

SIR – Could Messers Branson, Musk and Bezos travel to space on a one-way ticket?

Helen Penney
Longborough, Gloucestershire

Is it just me...

SIR – In keeping with most right-thinking people in this country I'd like to propose banning everything.

Carey Waite
Chailey Green, East Sussex

SIR – I have compiled below a detailed list of the benefits of Brexit to date.

Gavin Aldred
London SW6

SIR – I am now 37. I hope I live long enough to see some precedented times.

Dr Ian Coyle-Gilchrist
Foxton, Cambridgeshire

THAT'S
ENTERTAINMENT

Today's news

SIR – There seems to be no situation so dire that it can't be made worse by the BBC *Today* programme's reporting of it.

David Empringham
Warwick

SIR – Did John Humphrys take punctuation away with him when he retired from the *Today* programme?

Trevor Wye
Ashford, Kent

SIR – I am now convinced that the BBC is striving to win a BAFTA at the next awards for Best Dramatic Programme – the Six O'Clock News.

David Barnett
Newark, Nottinghamshire

SIR – I hope our PM and his colleagues realise their pep talks at 5pm on BBC One are massively counterproductive – in recent days *The Repair Shop* has been cancelled or rescheduled at least four times.

Derek Forster
Worthing, West Sussex

SIR – Channel 4 boss Ian Katz considers that his most important job is to cheer people up.

I have always been surprised that so many are upset by Channel 4 News. If viewed in the right spirit this programme, with its po-faced presentation, can be one of the funniest, coming in behind *Fawlty Towers*, *Yes, Minister*, *To the Manor Born* and *The Good Life*.

Frank Parkinson
Reading

SIR – The new GB News station may be a disappointment, but it is fine if you like the news read and discussed by people sitting in the dark.

David Tucker
Stokenchurch, Buckinghamshire

SIR – If Tim Davie, Director-General at the BBC, wants to increase diversity of perspective and opinion within his organisation, there's a cheaper and simpler way than migrating staff and operations to the North of England.

It's radical, I know, but he might consider placing BBC job advertisements in *The Daily Telegraph*.

Iwan Price-Evans
Croydon, Surrey

SIR – I have given up watching the lunchtime news on the BBC. I now watch *Tales of the Unexpected* on Sky Arts. It amounts to much the same thing really.

F. S. N.
Via email

Lure of the small screen

SIR – TV news producers and presenters should return to providing news, impartial commentary and sensible questioning. I am not interested in celebrity presenters' personal opinions.

However, I am looking forward to Piers Morgan's *Strictly* Argentine tango this autumn.

Christopher Hunt
Swanley, Kent

SIR – It is reported that Craig Revel Horwood wants Jeremy Corbyn to take part in this year's *Strictly Come Dancing*. As a dyed-in-the-wool Leftie, will he try the impossible; to dance with two left feet?

Stephen Howey
Woodford Green, Essex

SIR – Rather than listening to the people, Sir Keir Starmer should watch more telly. Look what it did for the Prime Minister as well as Ann Widdecombe and Ed Balls.

He would need to be selective. A strong performance in *Strictly* or a good run in *The Great British Bake Off* could work wonders. Appearing on *Pointless* or *Would I Lie to You?* might generate unfortunate headlines, and it would be suicidal to go anywhere near *Have I Got News for You*.

Involvement with programmes about railways, canals or restoring French chateaux might suggest he is thinking about a new career.

Peter James
Telford, Shropshire

Nights in with Auntie Beeb

SIR – With BBC One's back-to-back programmes on a Sunday evening (*Countryfile*, *Antiques Roadshow*, *Call the Midwife* and *Line of Duty*), when is a person supposed to eat?

Richard Quicke
Hazeley Lea, Hampshire

SIR – Your article headed "Luther 'lacks Caribbean authenticity'" makes me wonder whether I, as a second-generation Polish person, should stop eating fish and chips and take pierogi on board instead.

Henry Maj
Armitage, Staffordshire

SIR – Nish Kumar says he will never host another comedy show for the BBC.
    Let's hope that is a promise.

Andrew Babington
Belfast

SIR – I've just watched *The Great British Sewing Bee* tonight and it's had me in stitches.

> **A. L.**
> Via email

SIR – I never thought that I could be influenced by television but my wife tells me that, since *The Great British Sewing Bee* started, I have stopped saying "clothes" and started saying "garments". Guilty as charged.

> **Dave Alsop**
> Churchdown, Gloucestershire

SIR – After football flurries and tennis tantrums, does the arrival of *Only Connect* and *University Challenge* herald the advent of autumn?

> **Avril Wright**
> Snettisham, Norfolk

SIR – Lullabies sung are suggested for people who struggle to get to sleep to avoid them taking sleeping pills.

I find turning the light off and the day's episode of *The Archers* on does the trick.

> **Joanna Bunkham**
> Swansea

SIR – The Dyson Investigation seems to have concluded that the BBC needs a good going over with a vacuum cleaner.

> **Martin Hall**
> Welwyn Garden City, Hertfordshire

SIR – Now is the appropriate time for Lord Hall to revert to plain Mr Hall.

John Hinchsliff
Edgworth, Lancashire

SIR – The curmudgeonly and vastly unpopular decision by the BBC to axe the uplifting Radio 4 theme in favour of yet more news and current affairs was a sad move. Now there appears to be a glimmer of hope that it will be reinstated. Yes please! If you have to get up at the ungodly hour of 5.30am, you deserve a rousing start to the day.

Ann Cooper
Lytham St Annes, Lancashire

Noisy nature

SIR – Sir David Attenborough is encouraging us all to enjoy the peace and the sounds of nature. Alas when he and many others take us via documentaries to amazing places all over the world, they take an orchestra and chorus with them which frequently drowns out the wonderful sounds of life in forests and oceans which we would love to hear.

Maggie Down
Paulerspury, Northamptonshire

SIR – Heard on the *Today* programme at about eight-fifty-five this morning: "It's life, but not as we know it: on a rock, under three thousand metres of ice. Scientists have discovered some life forms clinging on down there.

One of them is Dr Huw Griffiths."

There's always someone worse off than you.

M. I.
Via email

SIR – Am I the only one who is not too fond of "The Lark Ascending"?

It starts off well and is quite enjoyable, but then goes on and on and on. Yet each year it becomes the nation's favourite on Classic FM. I am not a violent person, but that bird needs shooting.

Judith White
Mellor, Lancashire

The old ones are the best

SIR – I was three years old when my parents took me to see *Bambi*. Apparently I cried non-stop until after we got home.

I am now 82. Maybe I'll get over it one day, but I rather doubt it.

Rosemary Marshall
New Malden, Surrey

SIR – I can't be the only father of daughters who blubs uncontrollably every time he hears Jenny Agutter deliver the line "Daddy, my daddy" at the end of *The Railway Children*.

Better get the Kleenex in for the sequel.

Dr Tony McAllister
Hertford

Letter of the law

SIR – My husband's appraisal of the new series of *Line of Duty* – TMEA: Too Many Effing Acronyms.

Lynette Johnson
Udny, Aberdeenshire

SIR – I have always found the plot of Verdi's *Il Trovatore* preposterous and unfathomable. I now find that it is simplicity itself when compared to the current series of *Line of Duty*.

Wendy Shell
London N7

A hard act to follow

SIR – Your front page describes Stephen Graham as "Britain's most modest actor".

Let's face it, he hasn't got much competition.

Mike Hedges
Clanfield, Hampshire

SIR – It's tricky, isn't it, deciding how literally to take woke guidance on using actors to play roles that are written for people of a different colour or persuasion?

I still bear the guilt of playing a dead body in a village play, when the local undertaker had a perfectly good supply of real ones in his funeral home.

Nigel Johnson-Hill
Petersfield, Hampshire

TRAVEL IN
LOCKDOWN
BRITAIN

Freedom of movement

SIR — My free bus pass expires in February. Today I received a replacement valid until 2026. The covering letter tells me it is available for immediate use. If only!

Lee Goodall
Churchdown, Gloucestershire

SIR — During more than 20 years living on Dartmoor I found the key to safety when walking was to make eye contact with oncoming drivers. People find it awkward to run over somebody with whom they have had social contact.

Julian Tope
Portishead, Somerset

SIR — After my car battery was replaced this week, the date on the display had reverted to 4 January 2013. I don't think I will change it as when I enter that metal enclosure I shall be transported into a world where Prince Harry is happy, families are not split by Brexit, we can all hug each other without the risk of passing on a killer virus — and, best of all, I am eight years younger.

Rachel Coventry
Malvern, Worcestershire

SIR – My first sign of spring is when I see someone holding on to the roof of their car in the mistaken belief that it might blow away once the sun is out.

Robert Ward
Loughborough, Leicestershire

Bumps in the road

SIR – Will self-driving cars be smart enough to avoid potholes? If not, will they be clever enough to change a punctured tyre?

Philip Jordan
East Malling, Kent

SIR – Having been denied our annual skiing trip to Italy this year, I am fortunate that I am able to continue the slalom by avoiding countless potholes in our Cheshire roads.

William Warburton
Macclesfield, Cheshire

SIR – I am struggling to find the paragraph in the Highway Code where it says big, expensive cars always have right of way and are entitled to push in at the end of a queue. It seems to be the law in this neck of the woods.

Nairn Lawson
Portbury, Somerset

SIR – Before using smart motorways, we need to understand the four lanes:
- Outside lane is reserved for BMW and Audi drivers
- Centre lane is the safest motorway lane
- Inside lane is the second most dangerous lane
- Only use the hard shoulder if you are contemplating suicide

> **Brian Christley**
> Abergele, Conwy

SIR – I wonder how long it will be before the authorities start calling e-scooters "smart". That will, surely, make them safer.

> **Dr Michael A. Fopp**
> Soulbury, Buckinghamshire

Hell on two wheels

SIR – When I am on my bike, it seems to me that many pedestrians have little regard for cyclists. When I am walking, it seems to me that many cyclists have little regard for pedestrians. Which of me is right?

> **Dr Adrian Jacobs**
> Topsham, Devon

SIR – I was interested to read that cyclists shave their legs so that they can easily apply dressings, antiseptic cream and massage oil.

I usually need all those things as a result of shaving my legs.

Rita Coppillie
Liskeard, Cornwall

Track record

SIR – Michael Portillo should run Great British Railways. I look forward to the conductors' uniforms of red trousers and pastel blazers.

Mat Newman
Reading

SIR – Does the return of British Rail mean we will be subjected to a return of the British Rail sandwich?

Alan Whalley
Manchester

SIR – I wonder how long it will take before GBR will be taken to mean "Go By Road".

Brian Smith
Dunfermline, Fife

SIR – I am often confused by the train announcement urging me to take all my possessions with me when leaving the train. This is because I rarely take all of them on to the train in the first place.

Angela Clark
Tonbridge, Kent

Won't you come in?

SIR — To ensure that one had an empty seat alongside on any train journey, I was taught by my English lecturer (in the days of trains with compartments) to stand at the window with a faint smile, earnestly beckoning any would-be passenger to step inside.

It always worked.

Jane Moth
Snettisham, Norfolk

SIR — I found reading *The Daily Telegraph* often guaranteed the adjacent seat remained free.

I used to think my fellow passengers objected to my political views, but over time I came to the conclusion that they were wary of having a broadsheet waved in their face every time one turned the page.

Perhaps you could refer to this benefit when next advertising.

Richard Atkins
Pulborough, West Sussex

SIR — When passenger trains had compartments, I was told the best way of having a compartment to oneself was to peel an orange, throw the flesh out of the window and eat the peel.

Paul Saunders
Thame, Oxfordshire

Places to go, people to see

SIR — Perhaps Dull in Perthshire has a Dull Women's Rural Institute.

It certainly has a Dull Church.

Gordon Casely
Crathes, Kincardineshire

SIR — Apparently it has been claimed by scientists that Stonehenge is second-hand, having been somewhere else before. No wonder it hasn't got a roof.

Jonathan Batt
Castle Cary, Somerset

SIR — Surely the simplest solution to the controversy over the Stonehenge tunnel is to post the stones back to Wales.

John Skeeles
Hitchin, Hertfordshire

SIR — I read that, due to their mess, pigeons in Hungerford are to be relocated some 250 miles away.

Are we absolutely certain that they aren't homing pigeons?

Tony Parrack
London SW20

SIR – As a resident of Whitby I would be delighted to receive the pigeons, on the one condition that the good people of Hungerford agree to give a home to an equal number of seagulls.

Looking at my conservatory roof, I think I know which town would get the better deal.

Squadron Leader C. J. Carvell RAF (retd)
Whitby, North Yorkshire

HOME
THOUGHTS ON
ABROAD

Capitol offence

SIR – Would Donald Trump want to play golf with any of his "loved supporters" who attacked the Capitol building?

Keith Bolton
Chepstow, Monmouthshire

SIR – President Trump, the person with the nuclear codes, has been deemed too dangerous to have a Twitter account. I am not making this up.

Jeremy M. J. Havard
Chichester, West Sussex

SIR – If only impeachment could proceed as quickly as Twitter's suspension process.

Hon. Ian MacGregor
London N7

SIR – There are two types who habitually applaud themselves: chimpanzees and Donald Trump. (Chimpanzees are the happy ones.)

Ian Turnbull
Tunbridge Wells, Kent

Biden's White House bid

SIR – I note that the BBC correspondent Jon Sopel's eyebrows have returned to the correct position, following four years of being raised almost to his hairline on a daily basis in sheer incredulity at the events he has been called upon to relate.

> **Lynne Chilver**
> Uxbridge, Middlesex

SIR – When President Biden takes up residency in the White House, would it be a surprise if the previous occupant had removed all the light bulbs?

> **Jim Allpass**
> Marlow, Buckinghamshire

SIR – Biden has already proved useful. A tape of his acceptance speech is an excellent cure for insomnia.

> **Charlotte Joseph**
> Lawford, Essex

SIR – If the Prime Minister regards any 78-year-old delegate as "a breath of fresh air", he needs to either get out more or widen his circle of friends.

> **David S. Ainsworth**
> Manchester

SIR – "Indestructible relationship"; "unsinkable *Titanic*".

> **Edward Hill**
> Chandlers Ford, Hampshire

Land of the free

SIR – Many moons ago I was on an RAF detachment to South Dakota, USA. The hundred or so of us were given a briefing by the chief of police. A genial soul, who carried a massive silver-plated gun, he was very emphatic on two points. If stopped by the police do not resist arrest and make no sudden movements with your hands. Secondly, and more important, do not steal the US flag – Americans are very sensitive on this issue. I am not aware of any altercations with the police but, obviously, the massive town flag was gone before sunup the next day.

Wg Cdr John Grogan (retd)
Congleton, Cheshire

SIR – Television news footage today shows a Trump supporter in Washington brandishing a placard demanding the right to "BARE ARMS".

Strangely enough the protester himself wore long sleeves. Perhaps he was impatient for the vaccine.

Sam Kelly
Oldham, Lancashire

Naked ambition

SIR – The German chancellor Angela Merkel is suggesting that Brits be excluded from travelling to EU holiday destinations.

This looks like nothing more than a vote-grabbing exercise.

German beach-lovers could afford themselves an extra hour in bed before putting their towels out on the sunloungers.

Robert Barlow
Little Bookham, Surrey

Europe cut off

SIR – Should the EU ban the export of vaccines to the UK, I propose to ban exporting myself on holiday to the EU.

Sue Granik
London NW10

SIR – The AstraZeneca vaccine does cause clots: they sit around the EU table in Brussels.

Sandy Pratt
Storrington, West Sussex

SIR – Britain vaccinates while Europe vacillates.

Peter Kievenaar
Chelsworth, Suffolk

SIR – I don't think we need to worry about exporting our vaccines to the EU any time soon: just think of the paperwork.

Sarah Hellings Smith
North Berwick, East Lothian

Take me to your leaders

SIR – The President of the European Council should be renamed Frau Useless gone Delaying.

With much sympathy for the beleaguered subjects of the European Union,

William Prince
Brightlingsea, Essex

SIR – Ursula von der Leyen has been removed from my Christmas card list.

Ian Squires
Beckermet, Cumbria

SIR – I presume that Boris calls them "our European friends" in the same way as Mark Antony referred to Brutus as an "honourable man".

At least, I hope so.

John Frankel
Newbury, Berkshire

SIR – Could we crowdfund the defence of the person who slapped Emmanuel Macron?

Laurence Barnes
Tattenhall, Cheshire

SIR – The sight of Trump holding Mrs May's hand was bad enough – but Emmanuel Macron cuddling Joe Biden at the G7 summit was beyond the pale.

Malcolm Priestley
Great Missenden, Buckinghamshire

Avoiding a wurst case scenario

SIR – It was my understanding that the dispute with the European Union over sausages was resolved by the Rt Hon James Hacker MP immediately prior to his becoming Prime Minister.

Christopher Horne
Rickmansworth, Hertfordshire

SIR – Where are the enterprising sausage smugglers? Northern Ireland needs them.

Margaret Durrant
Sonning Common, Oxfordshire

France's power grab

SIR – I noticed that when you listed the food and drink due to be served to the G7 leaders there was no mention of any French wine or cheese. I do hope this exclusion is now the Government's official policy. (It is certainly mine.) I also hope we served proper British sausages to Monsieur Macron at the barbecue.

Sir Michael Ferguson Davie
Bath, Somerset

SIR – Like many readers I am appalled and exasperated at the way some French government ministers are threatening power to Jersey. I have taken appropriate action and swapped Brie de Meaux for Somerset Brie, Calvados for Somerset Apple Brandy and Muscadet for English wine.

Celia Wright
Sturminster Newton, Dorset

SIR – If the French complain about their share of our fish, then let them eat roast beef.

Tony Tighe
Devizes, Wiltshire

SIR – Clearly some high-level talks are needed urgently between Britain and France to resolve the fishing dispute. I suggest the wardroom of HMS *Victory* as a suitable venue.

Andrew Dyke
London N21

SIR – I am concerned for the French wine harvest.

In view of the French reaction to Brexit, and to the AstraZeneca vaccine, will there be a harvest of sour grapes?

Maurice Skermer
Banbury, Oxfordshire

Giants on the world stage

SIR — Following the recent French elections, it appears that President Macron is becoming President Micron.

C. Williams
Wrexham

SIR — Kim Jong-Un has apparently lost a lot of weight. I didn't know Jane Plan delivered to North Korea.

Jackie Mullens
Chertsey, Surrey

SIR — The Kremlin has passed legislation stipulating that the word "champagne" can only be applied to wine produced in Russia. Is this a new form of fizz-illogical warfare?

Jack Ryding
Trefnant, Denbighshire

SIR — Perhaps we can come to an arrangement with the Russians.

We will steer clear of Crimea if you do likewise with Salisbury.

Peter Kievenaar
Chelsworth, Suffolk

SIR – In line with the current mood I suggest that the Italians return the European Championship trophy to England in reparation for the invasion of AD 43.

Gordon Welford
Portishead, Somerset

Escape to any country

SIR – Presumably we are still allowed to leave the country in order to emigrate. If so, a move to North Korea is becoming more attractive by the day.

Graham Low
Malpas, Cheshire

SIR – I recently received a blank postcard. The sender said it was of all the places she hadn't been to in the last year.

Ian Cribb
Poole, Dorset

SIR – Perhaps the Government needs to differentiate between holiday-makers and those who have family living abroad. My husband and I would like to fly to Florida. We want to see our son. Not the sun.

Barbara N. Wakely
London SW6

SIR – Despite yet another expert giving me instructions to stay at home, I have been examining my options for a holiday from the Government's green list – options which I have to say are not encouraging.

Brunei? No alcohol permitted. South Sandwich Islands? Uninhabited. South Georgia? Uninhabited. Falkland Islands? Direct flights by courtesy of the RAF only. Singapore? New variant of Covid suspected. Israel? Danger from falling masonry. Australia and New Zealand? Borders closed to foreigners. Iceland? Too much volcanic ash in one's cornflakes. St Helena? OK only for retired military generals and direct flights only from Johannesburg on a Saturday. Ascension Islands? Uninhabited. Portugal? Full of Brits – so it looks like it's going to be the Faroe Islands again.

> **Martin Henry**
> Good Easter, Essex

SIR – My wife and I have been looking forward to a holiday in France this summer, planning to visit my mother-in-law for the first time in two years.

However, planning the trip has been a nightmare, as we try to second-guess where the goalposts might move to next and anticipate what chaos and unpleasantness might await us.

The Covid regulations look like they might cause some problems as well.

> **Martin Wynne**
> Oxford

SIR – I note that people entering this country from Peru will have to go into a quarantine hotel. Does this mean that Paddington will get a reduction on his food bill as he'll only require marmalade sandwiches to be left outside his door?

Dorothy Westman
Taunton, Somerset

SIR – Perhaps those who are intent on jetting off for a foreign holiday should be allowed to – as long as they sit by an open window on the plane.

Sue Milne
Crick, Northamptonshire

A disappointing note

SIR – Just when you thought things couldn't get any worse, we hear that the Eurovision Song Contest is going ahead.

Susan Lister
West Horndon, Essex

SPORTING
TRIUMPH AND
DISASTER

Come on, you Reds

SIR – In my marriage there were three of us. Me, my husband and Liverpool football club.

>   **Carmena Newey**
>   Liverpool

SIR – I had hoped that one good effect of social distancing might be the eradication of the childishly exhibitionist hugging that goes on whenever a professional footballer does what he is overpaid to do, namely, score goals. Alas!

>   **Ron Hurrell**
>   Benfleet, Essex

SIR – Anyone wishing to measure the strength of our Union need look no further than all four of our nations united in support for the Scottish team to beat France for the benefit of Wales – and not a politician in sight.

>   **Kip Calderara**
>   Chesham, Buckinghamshire

SIR – While binge-watching weekend football on television, I have found the easy answer to avoiding a goalless draw is to either fall asleep on the sofa or go out and make a cup of tea.

>   **John Hawley**
>   Ruislip, Middlesex

SIR — What a pity that the "beautiful game" has now developed into a martial art, condoned by football's ruling bodies.

Dr Frank Booth
Exmouth, Devon

SIR — The new England football logo must come as a great disappointment to all those lions who wish to self-identify as tigers.

Charles Smith-Jones
Landrake, Cornwall

SIR — The match last night was most interesting. I really enjoy watching grass grow.

Brian Birkenhead
London W1

A league of their own

SIR — As an Arsenal supporter I suppose I should welcome the formation of a Super League. On recent form it's the only way we're going to get to play the big Spanish and Italian clubs.

David Miller
Tunbridge Wells, Kent

SIR – With the world's most overpaid prima donna footballers confined to a solitary league of no consequence, banished from all other forms of domestic, European and world competition, along with the evidently arrogant clubs they represent, what's not to like?

The English Premier League would emerge more competitive and more exciting, with all clubs vying for success and fending off relegation on more equal terms.

Christopher Healy
Fridaythorpe, East Yorkshire

SIR – Of course the next logical stage would be for the top two clubs of the proposed European Super League to play against their counterparts from the soon-to-be-announced Super Leagues from each of the FIFA regions in Africa, Asia, South America, etc. The top clubs from *that* league then represent our planet in the Solar System League – but there may have to be a handicap system in place when the representatives from Earth come up against the eleven-limbed players from Neptune City One or the three-headed opponents representing Venus.

Alan Brown
Medstead, Hampshire

SIR – In the light of moves by the big European clubs, may I suggest that football reporting should now be moved from the Sport to the Business supplement?

It would seem a better fit.

Roger Mills
Chichester, West Sussex

SIR – In earlier, happier times, football was just a game.

Neale Edwards
Chard, Somerset

SIR – The Prime Minister's laudable proposal to ban the moronic individuals who racially abuse footballers from attending matches is to be applauded. It is a delicious irony that these people will be put on what will undoubtedly be referred to as a "blacklist".

Captain Graham Sullivan RN (retd)
Gislingham, Suffolk

Is it coming home?

SIR – Just when life could not have been more unprecedented, England have beaten Germany at Wembley.

Kirsty Blunt
Sedgeford, Norfolk

SIR – BBC headline? "In spite of Brexit, England 2: Germany 0".

Richard Brown
Heathfield, East Sussex

SIR — I was convinced that we'd had a mini hurricane just after 9pm this evening.

However, I soon realised it was the sigh of relief emitted by pub landlords all over the country as England's third goal went in.

Alan Mottram
Tarporley, Cheshire

SIR — If England loses the UEFA Euro 2020 final, life for those of us not interested in football will be unbearable; if it wins, life will be even more unbearable.

I am therefore planning a little trip abroad to somewhere where football is not discussed, and I will not have to self-isolate on my return.

I now understand why the Government has included South Georgia and South Sandwich Islands on its green list.

I'm off to pack my thermals.

Nicholas Young
London W13

SIR — I cannot wait for the England v Italy final on Sunday.

At least I can be certain that, on Sunday, I will have an uninterrupted view of the match. Unlike 55 years ago when my wife, then my fiancée, managed to arrange a dress fitting for her four bridesmaids starting at 3pm on World Cup final day and I was forced to accept my view of the screen being constantly interrupted by the parading bridesmaids. I think you can tell that I don't hold a grudge, 55 years on.

Stephen Wallis
Billericay, Essex

And now it's all over

SIR – I think the only ones smiling today will be the Scots and the EU countries.

Joan Manning
Barton on Sea, Hampshire

SIR – As soon as rumours emerged from No 10 that a Bank Holiday was in the offing if England won the Euros, Italy's win was guaranteed.

Paul Bendit
Arlington, East Sussex

SIR – *It's gone to Rome, it's gone to Rome*
Oh damn it, football's gone to Rome!

Jeremy Biggin
Sheffield, South Yorkshire

SIR – Italy may have won on penalties, but England won on daft haircuts.

Kenneth A. Anderson
Aston-on-Trent, Derbyshire

SIR – I have to apologise to the England football team. It was down to my lucky bottle of whisky that gave up too early.

Bob Shacklock
Onchan, Isle of Man

SIR – I'm consoling myself with the expectation of winning the World Cup next year. After all, it's something we do whenever the year ends with double numerals.

Margaret Croft
Liverpool

SIR – Never mind too much. We have the following to look forward to in the next few weeks: Lions v World Champions South Africa, England v Australia at cricket, the Olympics and the Ryder Cup.

Lots more opportunities for further disappointment.

Michael Upton
Nottingham

SIR – Some of the national anthems played and sung at the Euros are noticeably jollier than others. Should Britain decide to follow suit, I suggest that The Yetties be commissioned to give it the same treatment they have to the omnibus edition of *The Archers* theme tune "Barwick Green".

Bruce Denness
Niton, Isle of Wight

SIR – I would like to add a personal note of thanks to the entire England football team.

The stress and heartbreak related to the game resulted in an episode of chest pain and I have now been diagnosed with suspected coronary artery disease.

I am scheduled to have an angiography on Sunday.

My feelings of pride in the team and their great performance are as strong as ever.

I hope to be fitter to see them play in the World Cup final. And then they can bring football home.

Stephen Malnick, MA(Oxon) MSc MBBS(Lond)
AGAF MACG FEFIM
Via email

Golf on the wild side

SIR – When I played golf with my son in Australia there was a two-stroke penalty for hitting a kangaroo. When my son did so, the startled look on the roo's face and the humour of the situation reduced us to tears of laughter. And cost my son the game.

R. S.
Via email

SIR – The broadcaster Andrew Cotter, being unable to comment on normal sporting activities during the pandemic, took to giving running commentaries on his two dogs, Olive and Mabel.

In many ways Olive and Mabel helped to keep us sane. I appeal to him to continue so that our health and mental wellbeing can be maintained.

Jennifer Hammond
Broadstairs, Kent

SIR – The new Covid lockdown rules allow me to meet my friend at our golf course, and we can walk the fairways together for exercise, but were we to take a golf club with us and play the odd practice shot we could be arrested.

It's a funny old world.

M. G. Peaker
Northwood, Middlesex

SIR – Golf should be allowed during lockdown. With my slice I'm usually socially distanced from my playing partners anyway.

John Clark
Hereford

SIR – How I wish someone would do us all a favour, and find the moron who yells, "Get in the hole" after every golf shot at major competitions. Having found him (or her), a plastic bag could be placed over the offender's head.

David Kidd
Petersfield, Hampshire

Over and out

SIR – The English cricket team have been thrashed in India after a promising start to the series and the English rugby team has been thrashed by Wales after beating Italy.

Normal service is resumed.

J. S. F. Cash
Swinford, Leicestershire

SIR – I've coped with the Covid crisis without depression. Until the arrival of cricket's Hundred competition. Now I'm very depressed.

Anne Jappie
Cheltenham, Gloucestershire

SIR – I read that the game played with a bat and ball known as the Hundred competition is renaming wickets as "outs". Perhaps while they're at it, they could be persuaded to discontinue the heinous practice of calling it cricket.

Ronnie Cleave
Winkleigh, Devon

SIR – Simon Heffer tells us that limited-overs cricket involves "music, noise and drinking". I'm sold.

(Prof) Chris Barton
Stoke-on-Trent, Staffordshire

SIR – If cricket is ever to become acceptable to a wider global audience the rules need a change to allow the bowler, in his follow-through, to floor the batter in the latter's attempt to take a run.

Bill Hookey
Bookham, Surrey

SIR – For months I and – more importantly – my eight-year-old son have been looking forward to watching Somerset playing live at the end of June. Last night I received an email saying our tickets would be refunded due to prolonged restrictions.

This is just as well, as Sage's impeccable and infallible modelling showed that the match could last just 20 balls with no runs being scored, and thus would not be the spectacle we envisaged.

Charlie Bladon
Cattistock, Dorset

Water way to go

SIR – I read that "wild swimmers" have long complained about water quality in Britain's rivers.

I suppose that's the same as people who fancy doing chin-ups on the power cables of the West Coast mainline complaining about getting an electric shock.

Mike Owen
Claverdon, Warwickshire

SIR – We can all look forward to the Boat Race on Easter Sunday – but can anyone please tell me how it is that the same two teams always get to the final?

John Deeley
Burton-on-Trent, Staffordshire

Hands, face, ace

SIR – Watching the total lack of any social distancing at the tennis, I can only assume that Matt Hancock made the rules.

Richard Dalgleish
Newbury, Berkshire

SIR – Now that Andy Murray is doing so well with his new hip, I suspect they'll all want one.

Jacky Staff
Enniskillen, Co Fermanagh

SIR – Andy Murray has complained that the grass at Wimbledon is too slippery.

Next we'll have mariners complaining that the sea is too rough.

Ewen Southby-Tailyour
Ermington, Devon

SIR – Surely the strict dress code for competitors at Wimbledon is a classic example of white privilege.

Peter Lewis
Buckingham

SIR – It is a delight to hear that woollen sportswear is coming back into fashion for Wimbledon.

If only cyclists would shed their cockroach-like carapace and return to wearing wool – preferably in the form of tweed.

Jane Moth
Snettisham, Norfolk

SIR – I would suggest that Wimbledon would be a much more entertaining and agreeable spectacle if entry were to be restricted to players over the age of 65.

Derek Wellman
Lincoln

Talking points

SIR – I last watched Wimbledon when players had wooden rackets, didn't have chairs to sit on between games and there wasn't much squeaking or grunting every time a player hit a ball – although a TV commentator did offer "Ooh, I say" quite frequently.

Anne Jappie
Cheltenham, Gloucestershire

SIR – I wish that someone would come up with another adjective for a good shot at tennis.

They can't all be "unbelievable".

Sam Kelly
Oldham, Lancashire

SIR – Could someone please tell John Inverdale that
he is not being paid per word uttered.

D. R.
Via email

SIR – If the BBC's female Wimbledon commentators'
voices get much higher, only dogs will be able to hear
them.

Robin Baxter
Leigh-on-Sea, Essex

Podium finish

SIR – Commentators on the Olympics have invented
some new verbs with which to excite the pedants, as
in "He/she has medalled and will podium shortly".
Where will it all end? I'll think on it as I coffee.

David Shaw
Codford, Wiltshire

SIR – I understand that medal winners at the
Olympics are going to have to put on their own
medals, due to Covid restrictions. As the Olympics
are in Japan, surely they have a robot that could do
that.

Philip Roberts
Caernarfon

SIR – Next from Tokyo, the BBC will be bringing us affletics.

Charles Coulson
Quarrington, Lincolnshire

SIR – Those on the BBC commentatin' on the Olympics may have been trained by many of our current politicians like Priti Patel – who is in charge of policin' – and Sadiq Khan, who is runnin' London.

David Rapoport
Limpsfield, Surrey

SIR – As we now have skateboarding in the current Olympics and break-dancing in Paris, to attract a younger audience, surely Brisbane can celebrate its award of the 2032 Games by introducing "watering the garden" to attract us over-70s.

David Hall
Milton Keynes, Buckinghamshire

SIR – Freedom Day for me will be when the Olympics finally end and I can tune to the BBC in the mornings for local news.

Brian Earle
Felpham, West Sussex

SIR – Has something happened to our competitors in Tokyo, whereby if they win they cry and if they lose they cry?

Surely it won't be long before all the BBC commentators join them in a mass cry-in.

Philip Hall
Petersfield, Hampshire

SIR – Given Team GB's stunning success in Tokyo, I suggest that our entry for next year's Eurovision Song Contest be chosen from the pick of our Olympians. We've nothing to lose (quite literally) as musical ability seems neither essential nor, in many cases, even a requirement.

Alan Wiseman
Merriott, Somerset

ROYAL BLUSHES

Nothing like family

SIR — I see that Prince Andrew has a "crisis management specialist".

A job for life.

Greig Bannerman
Frant, East Sussex

SIR — You reported that the Earl of Wessex's job "just carries on relentlessly". Launching the odd ship and opening hospitals, all of which appear to be called Elizabeth, can hardly be classed as a burdensome occupation.

Michael Derrig
Twyford, Berkshire

SIR — From yesterday's Court Circular I read that "The Princess Royal this afternoon observed a Gloucestershire Constabulary Strategic Co-ordinating Group meeting via video link." Her Royal Highness has the patience of Job.

Lee Goodall
Churchdown, Gloucestershire

SIR — Thanks to your description of Princess Anne's cluttered, book-strewn, object-crammed sitting room as a "living room only the truly posh can pull off", I now have no hope of Marie Kondo-ing my parents' similarly stuffed house.

Alexandra Thompson
London SW17

SIR – If everyone who has ever styled themselves as "a cousin to the Queen" follows Her Majesty's example, a pretty high vaccination coverage should result.

Richard Weeks
Felixstowe, Suffolk

SIR – Monarchy may be hard to justify. I find, though, that saying "President Major" or "President Blair", for example, immediately cures Republican leanings.

Simon Longe
Beccles, Suffolk

Prince across the water

SIR – I was dismayed to see in your front-page photograph today that the Duke of Sussex can now no longer afford shoes or socks. I assume this is the price one pays for living in La La Land.

Grant Pryse
Harrogate, North Yorkshire

SIR – I was fascinated to learn from Prince Harry that Hollywood is the best place to learn to practise good parenting.

Ron Butcher
Great Dunmow, Essex

SIR – Congratulations to the Duke of Sussex on being appointed chief impact officer at BetterUp. Does this mean he has become a bouncer?

David Belcher
Thatcham, Berkshire

SIR – Prince Harry should take a leaf out of Tony Bullimore's book. When he was rescued in 1997 after being stuck under his yacht for four days he was asked if he was going to get counselling. He replied: "Don't be crazy, I am going down the pub."

Carry Hepworth
Petworth, West Sussex

SIR – Harry and Meghan have clearly spent far too long playing with the Queen's waffle-maker present for Archie. It's time they gave it back to him, if it's not broken from over-use.

Alex Fletcher
Sevenoaks, Kent

SIR – To lose one aide may be regarded as a misfortune; to lose several looks like carelessness.

Julian H. Down
Pewsey, Wiltshire

SIR – Meghan and Harry are bringing the fair name of Sussex into disrepute. May I suggest they change the title of their fiefdom to somewhere more appropriate such as California?

> **David Sherman**
> Life Member, Sussex County Cricket Club
> London N3

SIR – Could it be that "Haz" is the new diminutive for "has-been"?

> **Anne Price**
> Tewkesbury, Gloucestershire

SIR – I have always thought that the system of primogeniture was grossly unfair to younger children. The recent behaviour of the Sussexes is perhaps changing my opinion.

> **Martin Stoneman**
> Torquay, Devon

SIR – Jordan's decision to ban the media from reporting the antics of their maverick prince seems worth considering.

> **Brian Christley**
> Abergele, Conwy

SIR – Following the news that Prince Harry is to publish an intimate memoir, perhaps a meeting between him and Dominic Cummings could be arranged as they appear to have so much in common.

John Nicholas
Langport, Somerset

SIR – I see that Prince Harry is planning to write and create a new class of book: the moanography.
   I won't be reading it.

David Evans
Farnham Common, Buckinghamshire

SIR – I now understand why I'm having difficulty in getting my children's fantasy novel published: I should have married a prince.

D. C.
Via email

SIR – For a young man who wanted to be left alone to get on with his life, the Duke of Sussex is remarkably noisy and ever present in our lives.

Cherry Tugby
Warminster, Wiltshire

SIR – For goodness sake, can't the Duke and Duchess of Sussex leave the press alone?

Very Reverend John S. Aveyard
Castleford, West Yorkshire

SIR – There are two things that I am really looking forward to: the end of lockdown and the absence of a photograph on the front, or any, page of your paper of the Duke and Duchess of Sussex.

Christopher Thompson
Ross-on-Wye, Herefordshire

SIR – I am sure we all applaud the Sussexes' decision to take several months off following the birth of their daughter.

Perhaps they could extend their time off until she starts school, or leaves university, or maybe marries.

Michael Tyce
Oxford

SIR – Perhaps someone can point out to Prince Harry and his wife that the Queen who sang "I want it all" were not related in any way to his family.

Charles Smith-Jones
Landrake, Cornwall

Her strength and stay

SIR – Prince Philip: a life of service. Prince Harry: take note.

Elizabeth Edmunds
Hassocks, West Sussex

SIR – Do we really need all this discussion about whether William meant this or Harry's tribute said that? It's simply splitting heirs.

Jane Jennings
Dursley, Gloucestershire

SIR – There is really only one way to describe the Duke of Edinburgh's passing and his legacy.
99 not out.

Conrad Marais
Virginia Water, Surrey

SIR – At last we know what to do with the fourth plinth in Trafalgar Square.

James Fraser
Knowle Green, Surrey

SIR – A statue should be commissioned as a tribute to Prince Philip. A group of offended Bristolians – who would not prove hard to find – could then march the statue straight to the city's harbour and throw it in.

Roger Crombie
Eastbourne, East Sussex

SIR – During his life the late Duke of Edinburgh undoubtedly contributed many fine and admirable things to our nation. Even in his sad passing he gave us one final, wonderful, gift; namely a few hours at

least of respite from the inane self-advertising of the
BBC for its forthcoming programmes.

Michael Latham
Oakham

SIR – As an amateur boater in the mid-1970s, my
father was meandering Southampton Water on his
18-foot motorboat when Tannoyed from astern with
the words "Good morning sir, do you mind giving way
for the *QE2*?"

While delighted to read of the proposed new royal
yacht, and supporting the memorial that this would
represent to the long-serving prince consort, one can
only wonder how HMS *Prince Philip* would transmit such
a request.

Chris Chambers
Exeter, Devon

SIR – I sympathise with the Duke of Edinburgh, who
resented being unable to name his own children. I
was also unable to name my four children. The only
member of the family I was able to name was our West
Highlander dog. I named him Sam after a toddler I'd
seen at the family of the breeder.

C. G.
Via email

SIR – Many have been sharing anecdotes about Prince Philip recently, but I wonder how many can claim, like me, to have been given the middle finger by the Duke?

It was about 30 years ago and I was driving early on a summer's morning on the M4 around Windsor. The road was empty and I was on automatic pilot when a huge black Freelander roared up behind me and blew its horn. I nearly jumped out of my skin and as the car overtook me I uttered an expletive and waved my fist at the driver, which occasioned a huge smile and the aforesaid middle finger salute in return. As the car passed, something about the driver's silhouette triggered a memory in my brain – it was only when I saw the car's HRH licence plate that I twigged.

I've felt affection for him ever since.

John Williams
Cardiff

It's all in a name

SIR – In future years Lilibet Mountbatten-Windsor may be very relieved that her parents were not related to Catsmeat Potter-Pirbright.

Jackie Mullens
Chertsey, Surrey

SIR – I suppose it could have been Queenie.

Rob Dorrell
Bath, Somerset

SIR – What a surprise that Harry and Meghan's newly born daughter isn't named Oprah.

Kim Potter
Lambourn, Berkshire

SIR – If the Sussexes don't want it [Dumbarton] for their lad, can I have it? I am well-suited.

Chris Barton
Stoke-on-Trent, Staffordshire

SIR – Might someone perhaps consult J. K. Rowling as to whether Professor Dumbledore was bullied when a wee wizard?

Jane Moore
Cambridge

SIR – Surely, due to the risk of being mispronounced, it is worse to be called a count.

Gordon Moser
Barkingside, Essex

TV royalty

SIR – I have decided that the only way for me to watch Oprah Winfrey's interview with the Sussexes is to record it. That way I can pause it and run into the garden to scream.

Jane Cullinan
Padstow, Cornwall

SIR – I am pleased that the Queen's corgis escaped criticism.

> **Greg Gilbert**
> Louth, Lincolnshire

SIR – I managed to last half an hour of the Harry/ Meghan interview, then thought I'd prefer more of a documentary, so changed channels to *The Crown*.

> **Peter Kievenaar**
> Chelsworth, Suffolk

SIR – Poor Meghan thought she had been given the lead only to find that it was a walk-on role.

> **Joan Campanini**
> Twickenham, Middlesex

SIR – Imagining myself as a fly, I am in a dilemma. Onto which royal wall should I alight this week?

> **Wendy M. Barrett**
> Shepperton, Surrey

SIR – I sympathise with the Duke of Sussex when he said "the Royal Family literally cut me off financially" when he withdrew from the "firm".

When I left my job at a firm in Aylesbury, they did the same to me.

> **David Hasted**
> Haddenham, Buckinghamshire

SIR – This is beginning to resemble a rather posh version of *The Jeremy Kyle Show*.

Brian Ross
Bradford, West Yorkshire

SIR – As a husband I am supportive, considerate and reliable. My wife's recollections vary…

M. Whittington
La La Land, California
(Taunton, Somerset)

Stranger than fiction

SIR – I see that the Duke and Duchess of Sussex's interview with Oprah Winfrey has been nominated for an Emmy; however, there appears to have been a mistake, as the category is non-fiction.

Graham Darby
Bournemouth, Dorset

SIR – I think we all know who will win Best Actress. But could there be a British winner of Best Supporting Actor?

Julian Pullan
Bramley, Hampshire

SIR – Has "fake news" been rebranded as "my truth"?

Sue King
Sidmouth, Devon

SIR – There were three people in Diana's marriage. There is only one in Meghan's.

John Baker
Crayford, Kent

SIR – I would like to take this opportunity to thank Meghan, Duchess of Sussex, for her yearning for publicity. Her ability to insult our monarchy, rubbish our country and hijack the nation's much-loved Harry has given my fabulous 93-year-old mother-in-law a whole new lease of life.

Until this week, she was very infirm and almost void of conversation; now she is animated and can talk of nothing else but her utter disgust at her (the Duchess of Sussex's) behaviour and how she should never have been allowed to get away with it.

"I am now hoping to live until I'm 100", she remarked. "I don't want to miss what happens next."

Charlotte MacKay
Shaftesbury, Dorset

Diana memorialised

SIR – Would someone please explain why a statue of Clare Balding has been erected in Kensington Palace Gardens?

Simon Addy
Hindon, Wiltshire

USE AND ABUSE
OF LANGUAGE

Ladies and gentlemen, please

SIR – Would the Queen kindly instruct Prince
William not to keep on addressing her subjects as
"you guys": apart from anything else at least half of
them are dolls.

> **Ted Shorter**
> Tonbridge, Kent

SIR – Apparently it is no longer acceptable for railway
staff to announce "Ladies and Gentlemen". I assume
those who continue to do so will be no-platformed.

> **John Williams**
> Bradwell-on-Sea, Essex

SIR – In order to avoid distress among my feminine
colleagues, and the ignominy of an appearance
in front of a complaints panel, I have adopted
"Comrades" as a form of address. So far I have had no
complaints.

> **Brian Inns**
> Melksham, Wiltshire

SIR – Following your report that the words "master"
and "slave" are to be removed from computer science
textbooks, it is to be hoped that computers themselves
will now feel liberated enough to identify as non-
binary.

> **Kevin Eyles**
> Blackburn, Lancashire

SIR – Gender neutrality. It's all those continental nouns I feel sorry for – what will become of them?

Fiona North
London SW4

SIR – I woke this morning to an invitation from my younger offspring (the one capable of giving birth) to breakfast on Sunday 20 June – Sperm Provider's Day. I do hope I can have an egg.

John Miles
Ely, Cambridgeshire

SIR – If anyone refers to me as "the person who assisted in the fertilisation process" rather than the "father", they can expect a rather short, sharp and probably impolite response.

David Vincent
Cranbrook, Kent

SIR – I sincerely hope the "woke" brigade go back to sleep.

Gareth Jones
Plymouth, Devon

That's us told

SIR – A tribunal heard how "telling a grandma how to suck eggs" can be sexist. Surely, the case won't be decided until a fat lady sings.

Cameron Morice
Reading

SIR – Whenever anyone says to me: "Take care", my response is: "You have to, at my age".

David Bryce
Norwich

SIR – In response to an invitation to "Have a nice day", an old American friend would counter with "Sorry, but I have other plans".

Geoff Neale
Cheltenham, Gloucestershire

Put away childish things

SIR – We had kids on our lawns during the last World War. The pair of them ate my sister's dolls' house which she had unwisely left outside. The US soldiers billeted in our house referred to us as "kids". We did not appreciate this: we did not eat dolls' houses. Children are children and kids are baby goats, not human children.

Alexander Hopkinson-Woolley
Bembridge, Isle of Wight

SIR — I have just received an email from a reputable company advertising special treats for Mum's day.

I have learnt to cope with Mothering Sunday being referred to as Mother's Day but Mum's day is a bridge too far.

Amanda Howard
Enfield, Middlesex

SIR — Out of interest and necessity I have visited builders' merchants and DIY stores from an early age. In my teens, I was usually greeted with "Yes, lad?" In my twenties it became "Yes, young man?" and for a couple of decades in my forties and fifties I must have looked more respectable as "Yes, sir?" became more usual. It was downhill from then on, with "Yes, mate?" being the only form of address for the next 20 years or so.

Having now reached 70, I can report that I have been promoted to "bud". What next, I wonder?

James Farrington
Hartfield, East Sussex

SIR — When my daughter, like, started using the word, like, every other word like, I started to copy her every time we spoke, like.

She stopped the practice immediately — what a pity there's nobody, like, who can step up to the plate and help Prince Harry out, like.

Mike Forlan
Hayling Island, Hampshire

SIR – Some younger people seem to think that the *Telegraph* is read only by the elderly. A good way to combat this perception would be to start every headline with "So".

Just imagine. "So, hopes fade for end of lockdown". Thirty years younger, instantly.

Andrew Ingram
Maidenhead, Berkshire

SIR – I regularly take photos of inanimate objects issuing instructions: "Handle me with care", or apologies: "Sorry I'm not in service".

I then send these to my family as examples to support my increasing conviction that we live in Toy Town.

They are duly grateful.

Warwick Jones
Purley, Surrey

SIR – One should avoid anthropomorphising inanimate objects – they don't like it.

Patrick Holligan
Leicester

This won't hurt a bit

SIR – Seeing a white van driving out of a nearby dental surgery car park does not usually attract attention, but when it carries the sign "STUMPBUSTERS" one can only imagine the dentist needed serious help with an extraction.

Stuart Asbury
Blandford, Dorset

SIR – In Nature Notes, your correspondent refers to intact or "un-neutered male felines" as "toms".

Nowadays, we try to avoid language that causes offence to particular groups of society – and I find "toms" particularly insulting, especially when used in the same context as "castration".

Tom Suffolk
West Horsley, Surrey

It must be catching on

SIR – Should I have the misfortune to contract Covid-19, may I request that I test positively rather than test positive for the virus?

It would be a small comfort when most needed. Besides, laughter creates positive end airways pressure in the lungs; positively therapeutic.

Dr Timothy Davey
Bristol

SIR – No day passes without a report of something being "rolled out" – typically vaccines rather than pastry.

Chris Cleland
Farnham, Surrey

SIR – One aspect of German often remarked upon by those new to the language is its ability to express a fairly complex idea in a single, albeit sometimes rather long compound word. Here's one I just made up: *Spiegellosebartanschauungsmöglichkeit* (feminine, of course).

I'm sure you don't need me to tell you that this refers to the situation of being able to look at one's beard without the aid of a mirror – a deplorable state of affairs resulting from the neglect, during lockdown, of certain civilised practices, in this case shaving. Roll on normality, is what I say.

William Smith
St Helens, Lancashire

SIR – How good to see that the Government's dismantling of English grammar proceeds apace. What could be better than to "stay home" and listen to Matt Hancock eradicate the preposition?

Roy Calcutt
Thame, Oxfordshire

SIR – It didn't take long for the latest noun to be turned into a verb. On BBC Radio 2 at the weekend the presenter asked a guest if they had "vaccined".

Peter Knowles
Leigh-on-Sea, Essex

SIR – When is the RHS going to let us know what to do about the new pest that is now blighting our lives? I refer to the "uptick" that is multiplying throughout the country.

William Wright
Reigate, Surrey

SIR – The only thing more mealy-mouthed than the caveats "could be" and "up to" is when the two are combined into "could be up to".

Keith Macpherson
Clevedon, Somerset

SIR – I am now deeply worried that the worry lines on my forehead are turning into concerning lines.

Christopher Morris
Walsall, Staffordshire

To cut a long subject short

SIR – The one thing that keeps me going through this bizarre election campaign is Sir Ed Davey's pronunciation of "Liberal Democrats" – condensing six syllables into one. An impressive achievement.

Brian Cole
Robertsbridge, East Sussex

SIR – I see from your Business columns that Standard Life Aberdeen is changing its name to Abrdn. It must have been painful to have been disemvowelled.

Andrew Cave
London NW3

SIR – The decision by Standard Life Aberdeen to rebrand as Abrdn is rbbsh. It makes a lghng stck of a once-great Scottish institution.

Michael Forward
Northampton

SIR – I'm sure I am not alone in rejoicing in the reintroduction of that critical hyphen in "mini-series" which avoids a regular mental stumbling block.

Janet Newis
Sidcup, Kent

SIR – Here in Jersey we applaud the activities of the St Lawrence Ladies Action Group, whose members have long cherished the acronym SLAGs.

Hamish Marett-Crosby
St Martin, Jersey

Recipe for disaster

SIR – I have just bought a box of 12 sachets of cat food (for the cat). On the back of each sachet it states the contents as "KITTEN WITH SALMON IN JELLY".

If I was an old lady I would be confused and horrified.

Stefan Badham
Portsmouth, Hampshire

On the offensive

SIR — My late husband was obliged to write reports on the rugby team he coached. Google could not accept the position of "props", so that the team would be "ably supported by the prostitutes".

A. B.
Via email

SIR — Your report on what swear words are permitted in which categories of film has left me *******ing to fill in the ****ing words. Surely your readers are adult enough to understand the ***** *******s used in everyday conversation without having them ****** well redacted?

Jeremy Nicholas
Great Bardfield, Essex

SIR — One of your recent features used the word ass, as in the phrase "kicking ass".

Ass, as a contraction of arse, is an appalling mealy-mouthed Americanism and should be struck from the lexicon and erased from common usage.

Arse is an Anglo-Saxon word of real power; D. H. Lawrence knew a thing or two.

Reclaim arse – and declaim it proudly, ideally starting in the pages of your newspaper.

Dr Roger Grimshaw
Manchester

SIR – We are reminded that the Skripals and Navalny were poisoned by a "weapons-grade" nerve agent.

Can we stop using this absurd expression? "Spoil-your-day-" or "social-faux-pas-" grade nerve agent do not exist in my experience.

Dr John Urquhart
Bury St Edmunds, Suffolk

Best foot forward

SIR – I would be grateful if someone, possibly a football commentator, would tell me which of my feet is the front one.

Reg Beard
Horsham, West Sussex

SIR – Are there any experts, professors or scientists left who aren't "leading"?

Joe Greaves
Fleckney, Leicestershire

Say what?

SIR – I have long believed that the four per cent
failure rate of the oral contraceptive is due to
teenagers continually hearing broadcasters referring
to them as "aural" contraceptives.

Malcolm Shifrin
Leatherhead, Surrey

SIR – The small cathedral town of Wells in Somerset
gets an awful lot of weather – it is mentioned in every
weather report. I wonder what the weather is like in
Wales.

Elizabeth Judd
Weybridge, Surrey

SIR – The mispronunciation of "prescription"
as "perscription" leaves me feeling in need of
medication.

Peter Gardner
Hydestile, Surrey

SIR – There seem to be an awful lot of men who suffer
from "prostrate" problems.

R. Smith
Bristol

SIR — I suppose that it was inevitable that we would have to endure a blitz of "Wemberleys" across all media.

Tim Hadland
Northampton

SIR — Why do governments always have a reshuffle before they have had a shuffle?

Graham Jones
Tytherington, Cheshire

SIR — Has anyone noticed that we don't have problems any more? We all have "issues".

Maureen Edmond
Dover, Kent

SIR — We British being fundamentally honest people, it seems strange that the phrase "to be honest" is uttered so often. It must amount to hundreds of millions of unnecessary words expended each day as some people seem to use it in every second sentence.
I am, to be dishonest, not one of them.

Christopher Massy-Beresford
Frome, Somerset

Just the job

SIR – I watched a fine film last night, *The Dig*.

The credits featured someone called an Intimacy Facilitator.

As I have plenty of spare time now, I wondered if this is something I could turn my hand to.

Do I need an NVQ, or is a good memory sufficient?

Philip Saunders
Bungay, Suffolk

SIR – Sticks and stones may break my bones but words may get me sacked.

Richard Poynder
Tunbridge Wells, Kent

DEAR
DAILY TELEGRAPH

Getting the word out

SIR — I notice that the *Telegraph* accepts letters "by post, fax and email only". So all those years of learning semaphore at Guides were wasted.

Rachel Palmer
Rhayader, Radnorshire

SIR — I have always been led to believe that people who write to newspapers are cranks or pedants so I have never written.

In my 88th year I am told by my family that I now qualify.

Ordinary Telegraphist R. Croome R.N. (retd)
Bristol

SIR — Is it my imagination or have the content, range and quality of the Letters page improved dramatically during lockdown?

With the possible exception of this effort.

Nick Stewart
London SW6

Photo opportunity

SIR — I write at the request of my wife Michele. On page II of your newspaper you published a photo of George Clooney.

It has now been cut out for posterity and she would like to enquire when you will be publishing more.

Tim Burgess
Rostherne, Cheshire

I'm sorry, I'll read that again

SIR – When I saw your headline, "Mr Potato Head is half the man he was", I was seriously concerned. My wife has always referred to Alex Salmond as Mr Potato Head.

Peter Gamble
Cirencester, Gloucestershire

SIR – There are certain phrases I thought I would never see in print on the front page of *The Daily Telegraph*. Among these (and fairly near the top of the list) was "same-sex potato families".

Andy Ritchie
Loxwood, West Sussex

SIR – A report in today's *Telegraph* about the discovery of a huge dinosaur footprint in Yorkshire states that it was "made by a woman collecting shellfish". Makes me wonder where the poor woman buys her shoes.

Gordon Galletly
Halstead, Kent

SIR – You report that a plan by Jesus College,
Cambridge to remove a memorial to Tobias Rustat
because of links to the slave trade has been "opposed
by his ancestors". There's foresight for you!

Derek Wellman
Lincoln

SIR – Your headline "Egrets? We have quite a few
more" for the report on the increase of the egret
population was excruciating.
  I wish I had written it.

Tony Renouf
Woolhampton, Berkshire

SIR – The caption to your photograph on page eight
of today's paper unfortunately is lacking in several
respects. Firstly, it is the locomotive, not the train,
which is No1, Lord Roberts. Secondly, the train has
not left (the) Bo'ness and Kinneal Railway – it is still
on it. It may have departed from Bo'ness however.
Finally, the train (the part which is hauled by the
locomotive) consists of carriages constructed by
British Railways in the 1950s/60s. It is the locomotive
which was built in 1899.
  Fortunately, I will soon be able to get out more.

Jonathan Mann
Director, Launceston Steam Railway
Launceston, Cornwall

SIR — From *The Daily Telegraph*, 20 Feb 2021, Saturday section: "Foolproof Roast Beef".

"Method: Choose a roasting tin big enough to hold the beef".

My faith in the media has been restored.

Aura Hargreaves
Beckenham, Kent

Dead tree media

SIR — Having conducted extensive research into the subject during lockdown, I can reliably inform your readers that without doubt, *The Daily Telegraph* is the most flammable of all newspapers and as a consequence is unbeatable when it comes to lighting a log fire.

Iain Campbell
Crieff, Perthshire

SIR — Apparently, Rupert Murdoch now thinks that his newspaper *The Sun* is worthless.

I could have told him that 40 years ago.

David Conway
Theydon Bois, Essex

One down, more to go

SIR – Congratulations to the setter of today's Quick Crossword, who managed to arrange matters so that every across answer begins with the letter B. I am not sure whether (s)he is a genius, or just needs to get out more, but for the sake of his/her sanity, I hope (s)he does not attempt to achieve the same feat with the letter Z.

Charles W. Agg
York

Away on business

SIR – Alex in the Business section appears to be holidaying alone. Does this mean his wife is taking a staycation or merely enjoying having the house to herself?

Christine Ashton
Lytham St Annes, Lancashire

SIR – My husband and I are happily married for ten months of every year. The remaining two months have a less harmonious start to each day as the *Telegraph* incorporates the Business pages in the main body of the paper. He watches me reading the news, subliminally urging me to finish, with greater attention than a Labrador watching someone eating an ice cream.

Jacqueline Bonham
Lytham St Annes, Lancashire

All part of the service

SIR – During the lockdown I was ever grateful for the subscription vouchers: they reminded me which day of the week it was.

Warwick Banks
Ketton, Rutland

SIR – The Obituaries Editor should be congratulated on producing work which is so often laced with unexpected humour.

I had a laugh-out-loud moment at breakfast when I read that the "doughtiest defender" of David Britton, author of the "last book to be banned in Britain for obscenity", was the writer, Michael Moorcock.

Keep up the good work.

Jeremy Archer
Newport, Isle of Wight

SIR – Your obituary of Catherine Tennant (12 June) made me wonder what happened to Psychic Psmith who was a great favourite of mine. Advice such as "Beware of an encounter with a digestive biscuit" was always very helpful.

Judy Davies
Tenby, Pembrokeshire

SIR – I see in today's announcements that Harry Ball will be marrying Lucy Foote on 16 July.

I hope they will have a hyphenated married name. Congratulations.

James Logan
Portstewart, County Londonderry

No longer alone in thinking

SIR – Thank heavens for intelligent people who lift our spirits and increase our knowledge. Of those, three have often kept me from despair: Jacob Rees-Mogg, Charles Moore and Nigel Farage, not necessarily in that order.

Camilla Coats-Carr
Teddington, Middlesex

SIR – Allison Pearson talks so much informed common sense on such a variety of topics, why can't we have her as prime minister? Failing that, Boris's adviser.

T. Neil Cook
Goostrey, Cheshire

SIR – Reading, once again, another article by Charles Moore.

Please Charles – marry me?

(I hope my husband doesn't read this.)

Jayne Robinson
Andover, Hampshire